AMAZING AND EXTRAORDINARY FACTS

THE
ENGLISH
COUNTRYSIDE

THE
ENGLISH
COUNTRYSIDE

Ruth Binney

RP
RYDON
PUBLISHING

A Rydon Publishing Book
35 The Quadrant
Hassocks
West Sussex
BN6 8BP
www.rydonpublishing.co.uk
www.rydonpublishing.com

New edition published by Rydon Publishing in 2024

First published by David & Charles in 2011
Revised edition first published by Rydon Publishing in 2015
Reprinted in 2016, 2019

A CIP catalogue record for this book is available from the British Library.

ISBN: 978-1-910821-45-9

Printed in the Czech Republic by FINIDIR, s.r.o

CONTENTS

Part 2: The Living Countryside

INTRODUCTION

I t may not be 'exotic' but the English countryside is a truly remarkable place. So remarkable, in fact, that the most difficult part of writing this book has not been what to include but what to leave out. In making my choices I have taken my cues from the features of the landscape, and the plants and animals within it, that have mysteries to unravel, stories to tell or which live or behave in an unusual way. These are tales of ancient civilizations, of the way the land has been worked over the centuries, and of the way in which these activities have left their mark in everything from the ridges and burial mounds on the hillsides to prehistoric walls and stepping stones, springs, wells, crop circles and hedges. Caves, carvings and megaliths are included and even the animals that graze peacefully in farmers' fields have remarkable histories. There is treasure to be found too – hoards of it buried beneath farmers' fields.

As for the 'natural' elements of the landscape, much that is amazing and extraordinary has qualified for inclusion because it is unexpected, hidden from view or takes place during the hours of darkness. It would be hard to guess at the teeming life that inhabits an oak tree, the leaf litter in a woodland or even a humble cowpat – or the amazing night time habits of the otter and the communities of badgers that may even bury their dead. More visible for all to see are plants that are poisonous, edible, healing and invasive – and even some that have evolved lifestyles as parasites or carnivores. In the skies it is easy to marvel at everything from the high speed stoop of a peregrine falcon to a flock of more than 40,000 starlings heading for their roosts at dusk. I have not seen one, but there are many reliable witnesses of 'big cats' that may roam the countryside, often in broad daylight.

Then there are the numerous myths, legends and old country beliefs that inextricably link the fabric of the landscape with the people who have inhabited it since the end of the last Ice Age. Tales of witches abound, linked with such creatures as hares, bats and toads. Elves – and even nightjars – are believed to roam at night stealing milk from cattle or goats, while many trees have been accorded powers of magic and healing. Springs and wells were once the objects of pagan worship but, more prosaically, are the reason behind the siting and naming of many of England's villages. In fact a myth or superstition of some kind can be found to be associated with almost every aspect of the countryside.

One of my great joys is to walk in the English countryside, particularly in the beautiful county of Dorset where I lived for so many years and which contains so many examples of the strange and amazing. Learning how and why the landscape reveals so much about its history, and sharpening my senses to observe and appreciate more closely the ways of the natural world, makes these walks ever more rewarding. Writing this book has also redoubled my energy for the proper conservation of all the countryside contains, from hedges to harvest mice. My hope is that reading it will do the same for you.

My thanks are due to Robert Ertle and his team for their help in preparing and publishing this revised and updated edition.

Ruth Binney
Cardiff, 2024

PART 1:
THE SHAPE OF
THE COUNTRYSIDE

The Message in the Rocks
Fossils and where to find them

Even away from the seashore, the landscape of England can yield a large number of remarkable fossils. But even the most avid fossil hunter will be unlikely to have the luck of the carpenter's daughter Mary Anning who discovered one of the first known dinosaur skeletons – that of an ichthyosaurus – near Lyme Regis in Dorset in 1811 or of Neville and Sally Hollingworth who in 2021 made Britain's largest ever find of Jurassic starfish, including three new species, in the Cotswolds.

Wherever there is chalk it is likely that fossils can be found, since chalk is largely composed of calcium carbonate from the shells of creatures that inhabited ancient seas. Literally hundreds of fossil sea urchins, for example, were found in a Bronze Age barrow in Bedfordshire excavated in the 1980s and 90s. Like other fossils these have long been valued as lucky charms and have country names such as fairy stones, shepherds' crowns and sugarloaves.

Chalk cliffs and quarries can also yield considerable numbers of belemnites, known as thunder bolts, elf-bolts and elf-arrows from their cylindrical bullet-like shape and pointed ends. According to legend these were either the bolts of the Germanic thunder god Thunor or were the armoury of malignant elves intent on destroying both cattle and humans.

Stones of legend

Curled just like sleeping snakes, fossil ammonites – sea creatures that thrived

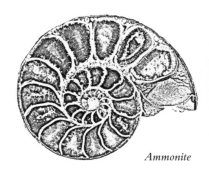

Ammonite

in the Jurassic some 100 million years ago – were once known as snake stones. Even in the early 18th century these were believed to have been formed in mysterious ways. In one typical story, they are said to have been created from snakes by St Hilda, the Saxon Abbess of Whitby, in the 7th century whilst she prayed.

In the same region of Yorkshire finds of the extinct oyster *Liostrea* and grooved shells of *Rhynchonella* are also common as are 'Devil's toenails' – which also look like oysters. These, carried in the pocket, are reputed to ease the pain of rheumatism. In Somerset, fossil hunters may easily find clusters of ancient corals known scientifically as *Lithostrotion* which resemble stone sponges.

HEALTHY CHARMS

Snake stones were held in greatest esteem by the Druids whose elders wore them around their necks. Sported in the same way, the stones were also believed to be able to prevent children from catching whooping cough.

Pictures in the Rocks
Shapes and illusions in the landscape

In many places in England, but particularly in areas such as the Peak District, stony outcrops in the landscape take on shapes and forms that can assume almost human proportions. A prime example is the Winking Man, which, when seen in profile juts out from Ramshaw Rocks on the road between Leek and Buxton. Driving north, changes in the light penetrating cavities in the rock make the 'eye' on the 'head'

The Winking Man

appear to wink. At Alderley Edge in Cheshire the face of a wizard stares down from the rocks, having once, it is said, filled a farmer's pockets with gold. Not only that, he supposedly struck a crack into the rock, which is there to this day.

Also in the Peak District the rocks of the Roaches make a shape that looks like a breaking wave. Further south in Shropshire are the Stiperstones, which contain a rock formation called the Devil's Chair. Legend has it that the Devil was flying over the area with an apronful of stones but slipped, letting his load fall to earth and so created this seat. Where part of the rock formation fell away, the Devil's window was made. It is also said that the ghost of Lady Godiva can be heard as she rides over the Stiperstones at night.

In Yorkshire, on Ilkley Moor, the Cow and Calf (also known as Hangingstone Rocks) jut from the land – one large, the other much smaller. According to local rumour there was once also a bull accompanying them, but he was quarried for his stone when the town of Ilkley was founded. The calf, it is said, split from the cow when the giant Rombald was fleeing from his angry wife and stamped on the rock as he leapt across the valley.

Used in the Stone Age – Discovered Today
Finding flint tools

Flint has been called the 'steel of the Stone Age' and in ancient England was used for a multitude of tasks – felling wood, killing animals and butchering their meat, building homes and attacking enemies.

Remnants of this Stone Age past can be found in many places, and almost anywhere in England it is possible to find a flint that has obviously been knapped or chipped and shaped, probably to give it a sharp edge and make it fit neatly into the hand.

Flint is made from crystalline silica, found in layers among limestone and chalk, and is black, grey or brown, often with a white patina on the surface where silica particles are concentrated. Areas around flint mines can yield good finds, as can ploughed fields around Bronze Age barrows, since flint was still used by ordinary people for centuries after bronze was first smelted.

The oldest flint tools yet discovered are from Swanscombe in the Thames Valley and were used some 400,000 years ago by Britain's earliest post-Ice Age populations, who predate *Homo sapiens* and were probably relatives of Neanderthals. However these, and simple tools or eoliths of a similar age found in locations such as Grays in Essex and Crayford in Kent were most probably shaped initially by the forces of nature in places where flint 'pebbles' formed in gravel and could simply be picked up from the ground and used immediately.

The most ancient 'true' flint tool is the hand axe, a stone that is roughly heart shaped with flakes of flint removed from the entire surface on each side. This would have been used for the kind of tasks for which

Flint tool

we would today employ a kitchen knife. However it would certainly not have been able to fell a tree. In a dig starting in 2021 near Frindsbury in Kent some 800 stone tools were unearthed including the third largest giant hand axes ever to be discovered. Measuring nearly 30 cm (1 ft) long it weighs over 31.6 kg (3½ lb).

Digging for flint

From around 6000 BC flint was mined in England, nowhere more successfully than at Grimes Graves in Norfolk where funnel-shaped hollows in the Brecklands are still evidence of this activity. Here, using flint axes, deer antlers and the leg bones and shoulder blades of oxen, our Neolithic ancestors dug round shafts up to 12m (40ft) deep to extract the material they needed for everyday life which, having been less exposed to the air, was harder and more durable. Suffolk and Surrey are other counties containing the remnants of flint mines.

Ancient Waves
'Reading' the ridges on the hillside

On country hillsides, in low light, one of the most spectacular sights is that of regular ridges running like waves across the land. These are not a geological phenomenon, but the signature of ancient agriculture. In Bronze and Iron Age Britain, these hillsides were fields ploughed with oxen and used to cultivate grains. Over the years, the soil became disturbed and slipped down the hillside to produce ridges known as positive lynchets (land reduced in level form negative lynchets). And while some archaeologists think that their formation was assisted by the weather, plus the effects of gravity, which would have loosened the soil, others believe that lynchets were in fact deliberately created to prevent such slippage.

As well as being ploughed, hillsides like these were also dug by hand in a system called cord rig. In Neolithic times, spades were used to excavate raised banks for cultivation with channels running alongside for drainage, and remains of ancient settlements are often found nearby in the form of stones of various kinds.

In other places, where the land was a little more easy to cultivate, ridges and furrows can also be made out. These are relatively recent, dating to ploughing in the Middle Ages. Because ploughs of this period were single sided, it was impossible for them to turn and plough along the same furrow. Instead ploughing was done clockwise, around a rectangular strip. As years went by, the soil became heaped into ridges, which farmers encouraged because it helped to improve drainage. These are visible today because the land was eventually returned to pasture for grazing.

FIRST FIELDS
On chalk uplands that have not been cultivated since Roman times it is possible to discern the pattern of fields that covered vast expanses. These were small and squarish, often surrounded by large banks. They bear the marks of ancient ploughing and were probably created in the Bronze Age. Many have been dated from shards of pottery – the lasting left-overs of ploughmen's lunches.

The Dead Lie Here
*Barrows of different shapes
and sizes*

From around 5,000 years ago until Anglo-Saxon times, it was the custom in England for people of power, reputation and renown to be laid to rest in tombs over which earth was piled to create burial mounds or barrows. Thousands of these still remain, chiefly in hilly areas such as Salisbury Plain, the Berkshire Ridgeway and Dorset's Purbeck Hills. Collectively known as tumuli they lend an air of ancient mystery to the landscape.

Oldest of all barrows are the long barrows, made from about 2300 to 1800 BC. Up to 91m (300ft) long by 30m (100ft) wide and 3.5m (12ft) in height these began as small rectangular mortuary enclosures of earth banks topped with timber palisades. Within was a room-sized mortuary chamber, supported by wooden posts, into which bodies were laid. Up to 50 men, women and children were placed in each, possibly with their possessions, although the evidence for this is slim. Finally, the chambers were surrounded and covered by large stone cairns – or might even have been set alight. At some sites, such as Wayland's Smithy in modern Oxfordshire (previously Berkshire) and at West Kennet in Wiltshire, long barrows were constructed with stone chambers made with huge stone slabs.

Later designs
Simpler than long

Neolithic chamber

barrows, and dating to the middle Neolithic, bank barrows take the form of long, sinuous, parallel-sided mounds, more or less uniform in height and width, and usually flanked with ditches on both sides. These do not contain chambers and may be the result of several phases of construction but are interesting for their rarity, existing at fewer than ten sites in England including Maiden Castle in Dorset and Long Low near Whetton in Staffordshire.

The bell barrow is typical of the Bronze Age, taking the form of a circular mound or mounds within a circular ditch, the mounds being separated from the ditch and each other by a flat space or collar known as a berm. An additional bank, outside the ditch, may also have been built. Unlike earlier barrows, bell barrows often contain grave goods such as daggers and pottery vessels, which would have contained food to nourish the departed. Here bodies would be buried, and later ashes, following cremation.

OTHER USES

Because of their height and prominence tumuli have been used in more modern times for many purposes – as sites for beacons and windmills, and even for gallows. In some places they were the setting for monthly open air courts.

Here Be Giants
Immense chalk figures

As well as horses, human figures have been carved into England's hillsides. Most famous of all is the massive 54m (180ft) Cerne Abbas Giant in Dorset, drawn brandishing a huge club and complete with face, nipples and ribs and displaying his massive manhood. He is now thought to have been created sometime between AD 700 and 1100, representing the Roman god Hercules and sited on a mustering point for Anglo-Saxon troops combatting Viking invaders. He was later adopted by Christians as a saint. Until 1635 a maypole was set up near the giant each year and today couples still make night time pilgrimages to the giant to make sure that their marriage will be blessed with children. Women who roll over the giant's appendage are believed to have their fertility doubly ensured.

In Sussex a similar but even larger figure reaching 9m (226ft) can be found. The Long Man of Wilmington on Windover Hill on the South Downs has origins that are equally obscure. The most recent theory is that he is a Saxon warrior god, and that he originally 'wore' a horned helmet which was subsequently turfed over by early Christians. Another story is that he represents a giant who was slain in a battle with another giant.

Legends in their Hooves
Horses carved on the hills

The art of leucippotomy, the carving of white horses into chalk uplands, can be witnessed in many parts of England, from Westbury in Wiltshire to Kilburn in North Yorkshire. The more modern of these horses (many date to the 19th century) were made for a variety of reasons from commemorating the departed to sheer creativity. Where old horses have been obliterated by neglect, as at Pewsey, new ones have even been made in their place.

Why horses? In Anglo-Saxon times, the invaders Hengist and Horsa are said to have fought under the standard of a white horse, while in the 18th century the white horse was a heraldic symbol of the British Royal Family, the House of Hanover.

Probably the most ancient hill carving in Britain, and unarguably the most striking of all England's white horses, is the graphic almost abstract figure at Uffington on the Ridgeway in Oxfordshire. Created by cutting trenches and filling them with chalk, the horse measures 115m (377ft) long and stands 33m (108ft) high. It may well date to the Iron Age, and to a tribe wishing to 'advertise' its territory. Certainly by the 1st century BC coins were being struck bearing its image. The horse also has legendary associations. On Dragon's Hill, a piece of land near the horse, St George is said to have slain the monstrous dragon, piercing its eye with his sword.

As at Pewsey, the Westbury White Horse is a replacement of something much more ancient. The original horse was cut below an Iron Age hill fort in the 1st millennium AD, but its origins are obscure. One theory is that it commemorates King Alfred's victory in the Battle of Ethandune in 878, although this is much disputed. In 1778, a certain George Gee, steward to Lord Abingdon, had the horse re-cut to a design nearer to its present day. A century later the horse had become misshapen and in 1873 it was restored once again.

The newest horse

Inspired by the Uffington White Horse England's newest creation was completed in Folkestone in 2003 near the entrance to the Channel Tunnel. Made of limestone slabs it was designed by the artist Charles Newington and constructed by a team of volunteers and Ghurkhas. The eye of the horse is placed over a point on the earth believed to radiate positive energy. In May 2004 a time capsule was buried behind the horse's heart.

The Uffington White Horse

The Most Ancient Enclosures
The story of walls

The walls that criss-cross England's countryside rank among its very oldest structures. In the Cotswolds a dry stone wall dating to 3000 BC still exists in a long barrow near Winchcombe, while in Cornwall the countryside is still divided by the walls created by farmers of the Bronze and Iron Ages to confine animals and crops. Although these have been displaced and modified by later field systems, the most ancient remain standing on the fringes of the Cornish uplands in the far west of the county.

These ancient walls were also made to a distinct pattern, with parallel walls, often miles long, intersected at irregular intervals by cross walls. In other places, particularly on heathland and chalk downlands, as in Dorset, Hampshire and Sussex, walls were used for confining smaller 'Celtic' fields and are thought to reflect the Iron Age practice of ploughing in two directions at right angles rather than one, as is usual today.

The art of wall making

The oldest Iron Age walls were made simply by creating banks of earth around large boulders then topping these with smaller stones and additional soil. However most of

Dry stone wall

the walls that still exist today are, like hedges, a legacy of the 18th century, when landowners began enclosing for farming areas that had previously been 'common' to country dwellers.

When it comes to skill, the art of dry stone walling, free of mortar is remarkable. The wall is built on a base of small stones laid within a trench and constructed so that every stone 'does its duty by its neighbour', meaning that even if the foundation were to sink the wall would remain intact. For easy passage of humans, old walls often have steps integrated into them. In upland areas such as the Yorkshire Dales, square openings or 'sheep creeps' are left in the lower part of the wall, just large enough to accommodate a single animal. Or the wall may even be built with removable stones or – 'cow creeps' through which cattle can pass.

LIVING DATE LINES

Because lichens can survive on walls and other rock surfaces for thousands of years they can be used to date a wall. The more compact kinds such as **Caloplaca heppiana,** *a common orange-yellow lichen of old walls will grow only 1–2mm (¹/₁₆in) every year, making it extremely valuable for the purpose. Leafier lichens will increase in size by about 10mm (²/₅in) per annum.*

Life on the wall

Some plants such as maidenhair ferns have a remarkable ability to grow in the gaps in walls, being able to survive with minimum soil, while on old walls a wild lettuce, a forerunner of the garden salad plant, will grow vigorously. Wall crevices create shelter for lizards which feed on woodlice, centipedes and the springtails which in turn use mosses and lichens for food. Up to 60 spider species are known to inhabit England's walls, including zebra and wolf spiders; walls are also home to harvestmen. A now rare butterfly, the wall brown, will bask in the warmth of a sunny wall and even has wing markings that look rather like bricks.

Stepping Stones of History
Crossing rivers and streams

Even from Neolithic times, pack horses – and humans – crossed rivers and streams at fords, making them hallmarks of the country's most ancient highways. And they were most necessary, for the Stone Age was one of great industry, with

Tarr Steps

materials such as flints being carried long distances across the land. Where a river was deep, stepping stones were often added or, as at Tarr Steps on the river Barle in Exmoor in around 1000 BC, a clapper bridge might be built, consisting of 17 stone slabs resting on stumpy granite 'pillars'.

Fords remained vital to transport in Roman and Anglo-Saxon England, especially in areas such as present day Oxfordshire (hence its name) where rivers were reasonably shallow. However clapper bridge construction was revived in medieval times, with bridges such as the one at Postbridge on Dartmoor being made wide enough to allow small carts to cross with relative ease. Often packhorse bridges were built alongside fords,

and a sure sign of an ancient pathway is one where the two exist alongside, although the surviving stone bridge may well be a replacement of an earlier construction, possibly created in Roman times then left to deteriorate beyond repair.

CARRYING THE DEPARTED

Stepping stones might also be used for carrying the dead. Across the river Tavy on Dartmoor leading to Lydford church, corpses were carried on stones laid so as to allow bearers to progress with their loads two by two.

Now You See Them ...
Streams that come and go with the seasons

In chalky areas, streams full to the brim with water in winter may disappear completely in summer, leaving behind only a line of willow trees, some reeds, irises or some clumps of watercress – either the 'real' variety, or fool's watercress, a relation of carrots and celery. Streams such as these are known as winterbournes, named from the Anglo-Saxon word for a stream flowing from a spring. In autumn, when the water table rises, the chalk below stream bed level begins to release its moisture back into the water courses. By spring, eggs of creatures such as dragonflies laid in the summer and kept in suspended animation during the dry months, hatch and feed.

Dragonfly

Winterbournes have lent their names to many villages: in Dorset they include Winterbourne Monkton, Winterbourne Zelston and Winterbourne Abbas, in Wiltshire Winterbourne Bassett and in Gloucestershire Winterbourne Down and simply Winterbourne. However in Kent they are known as nailbournes and in Yorkshire as gipseys. The unexpected, sudden revival of a winterbourne was recorded in 15th century Hertfordshire to be the signal of a forthcoming battle, crop failure or a deadly epidemic.

Craters in the Chalk
How rain makes holes in the ground

In a chalk or limestone landscape, a walker may come across a whole series of pits shaped like small craters with steep sides and rounded bottoms measuring from a few centimetres to hundreds of metres across. These are swallow holes, also known as sink holes, dolins or slockers, created by the action of weak acid in rain water that has run off vegetation or acid rocks. Or they may be created by river water, in which case the streams through which the swallow holes originated sink below ground.

In old swallow holes, where a stream has descended out of sight below ground, vegetation – including full sized trees – may grow lushly. In some landscapes, spaces and caverns develop underground as the rock dissolves. These sinkholes can be dramatic because the surface land usually stays intact until there is not enough support, then collapses dramatically, creating caves and cavities.

One of England's greatest concentrations of active swallow holes is along the river Mole in Surrey, in the heart of a chalk landscape, where some 25 active holes have been identified, some in the river bed itself, others on the river bank, yet others on the flood plain adjoining the river. When the Dorking to Leatherhead railway was being built in 1859 a fossilized swallow hole was discovered – proof that they have been forming for millennia.

Tracks of the Memory
Ley lines – and what they may mean

I n 1921 the 65-year-old Englishman Alfred Watkins was riding his horse over the hills of Brewardine in Herefordshire when he was suddenly struck by an intimate connection – a kind of invisible energy – between the past and the landscape. This sensation, which he called a 'flood of ancestral memory', was Watkins' perception of the system of ley lines. What he saw, later reinforced by consulting maps, was a connection between various prehistoric places, including standing stones, churches, burial mounds and other earthworks, all connected by straight lines running for miles across the countryside.

Salisbury Cathedral

The word ley is Anglo-Saxon and means 'cleared strip of ground' or 'meadow'. Watkins' theory was that they were old traders' tracks laid down by surveyors in the Neolithic, running from hilltop to hilltop, mountain ridge to mountain ridge, over the tops of valleys filled with dense forest. Over time this was cleared along the course of the straight tracks, or so he maintained.

Many leys have since been discovered by researchers such as John Michell who distinguished 22 alignments between 53 Neolithic and Bronze Age sites around Land's End in Cornwall. Other leys that can still be discerned includes one running for 30km (18 miles) linking Stonehenge on the Salisbury Plain in Wiltshire with an Iron Age fort at Old Sarum (the site of the original settlement of Salisbury), Salisbury Cathedral, an Iron Age camp at Clearbury Ring and another fort at Frankenbury Camp.

The scientific explanation of ley lines is that they are regions in which the magnetic field has been altered in some way, possibly through the presence of the mineral magnetite. However some people believe that, following the 'laws' of geomancy or placement, prehistoric people were aware of the presence of cosmic lines under the earth and built sacred structures along them in order to tap into their magical properties. To back up this theory they argue that many ancient groves, worshipped by the Druids, are sited on leys.

All Human Life is Here
The legends of England's standing stones

In the late Stone Age farming communities around England began erecting henges. Within the confines of a circular ditch and bank containing one or more entrances, wooden posts or stones were erected in different circular arrangements and sometimes in avenues. Most famous of these is Stonehenge (see p 28) but there are many other henges in other parts of England. And their purpose? All kinds of uses have been ascribed, from being places of worship to calendars and even dining areas.

Larger and older than Stonehenge, Avebury in Wiltshire is thought to date to 3000 BC. From the way in which triangular and columnar stones are paired, combined with evidence from burial pits within, the conclusion is that it was used for fertility rites and to mark the cycle of birth, life and death. Erected in a well-populated area, Avebury is thought to be aligned with Silbury Hill, a huge nearby burial mound some 40m (130ft) high, and with other smaller burial mounds nearby.

When first constructed there were originally some 400 stones on the Avebury site, with the heaviest, the Swindon Stone, weighing about 65 tonnes, and all of them transported from the nearby Marlborough Downs on wooden rollers. The outer circle, around the inside of the henge, originally comprised approximately 98 stones. Within this circle were two further circles of equal diameters. At the centre of the southern circle was an obelisk 6.4m (21ft) high while the northern circle was made up of a ring of 27 stones (only 4 survive today). Within it was a smaller circle surrounding a central cove thought to be aligned with the moon's most northerly rising point.

Smaller but equally impressive circles can be found at Castlerigg in the Lake District and at Merry Maidens in Cornwall where legend has it that the 19 stones are girls punished by being turned into stone for dancing on the Sabbath. North of Penrith in the Eden Valley is Long Meg, a slab of sandstone some 3.5m (12ft) tall supposedly a witch transmogrified for similar misdeeds. At the winter solstice, Meg's shadow becomes aligned with the 58 other stones – known as her daughters – with which she shares a huge circle.

Avebury

Stonehenge

The Ultimate Temple
Stonehenge – site of worship and celebration

About 4,500 years ago people of the late Stone Age began digging a vast henge – a circular ditch and earth rampart – on which were erected massive timber uprights. Some 400 years later here, on Salisbury Plain, the first of the 60 blue stones arrived from the Preseli Mountains in Wales by sea and land on rafts and rollers. So Stonehenge was 'founded'. In the 300 years that followed huge sarsen stones from the Marlborough Downs were added and arranged in a circle, with pairs of stones capped with lintels, the uprights cleverly sculpted so as to accommodate them securely – like very basic mortice and tenon joints. At this time the bluestones were

removed and eventually re-erected within the inner circle.

Stonehenge is arranged in two circles with an Avenue, a processional route lined by stones, leading to the river Avon. The entrance of the outer circle is aligned with the midsummer sunrise, suggesting that the purpose of the whole was sun worship, and today Druids gather there at the summer solstice for just this purpose. Other theories are that it was some kind of astronomical 'instrument' for calculating the movements of sun, moon and stars, and for predicting eclipses. However the many burial mounds situated nearby suggest that it was more likely to have been used to commemorate rites of passage.

The newest discovery
Some archaeological investigations carried out in 2010, made using

the most advanced techniques of geophysical imaging, have revealed evidence of another henge alongside Stonehenge and dating to about 2500 BC, of the same size and only 900m (½ mile) away, made of wood and set in place with exactly the same orientation to the sun. Within is a burial mound. Current theory is that it could have been a burial site or even a place for hosting feasts to celebrate the lives of the departed. In 2014, researchers employing ground-penetrating radar discovered a pair of huge pits in a previously unknown monument called the Cursus. Not only does this predate Stonehenge by 400 years, but the pits are situated so that the place where their alignments intersect at sunrise and sunset respectively mark the point where Stonehenge was erected.

Excavations in 2021 revealed Neolithic and Bronze age human remains and artefacts including grooved pottery and a shale object that could have been part of a club. In the Preseli Hills of Pembrokeshire a newly discovered a bluestone monument is not only remarkably similar to Stonehenge but nearby

empty stoneholes correspond remarkably well to particular stones (dolerites) at Stonehenge.

If Trees Could Talk
How to date an English hedge

Hedges are England's biggest nature reserve, but one that is in constant danger. Uprooting of hedges by farmers to create ever larger fields peaked in the mid 1960s with an annual loss of about 16,000km (10,000 miles), and although the rate of destruction has slowed considerably, nearly a third of England's hedgerows have disappeared within the lifetime of the current adult population.

The pattern of hedges that exists today dates largely from the 18th century, when the Enclosures Act put an end to common land and when, in the years between 1750 and 1850, some 322,000km (200,000 miles) of hedges were created. But English hedges have a much longer history, the oldest dating to the Neolithic.

Bronze Age hedges were used as boundary markers and the Anglo-

Saxons were also hedge-builders. Charters of the time mention permanent hedges, often with individual, named trees standing in them, and designated to the specific purpose of enclosing deer. As well as demarcating fields, many of these ancient hedges marked the boundaries of woodlands; they were most common in Worcestershire, Hampshire and Oxfordshire – a pattern that still corresponds to hedges of today. Hedge planting continued in Medieval times as well as the creation of 'dead hedges' consisting of stakes set about 60cm (2ft) apart and interwoven with flexible branches.

The age of a hedge

Today, as in times past, the most common hedge plants are hawthorn, blackthorn, and hazel, plus holly, beech, oak, ash and willow. However an old hedge contains many more different species than this and in 1974 Dr Max Hooper published his rule for the dating of hedges – the result of a survey of more than 20 years. His 'formula' states that a hedge's age can be calculated by counting the number of different woody species, then multiplying by 110 years. This is fine as far as it goes, but can be confused by counting (or not) woody climbers such as ivy and brambles, which can throw out the calculation by a couple of centuries. And despite the fact that a living hedge with 13 woody species has been found in Suffolk, the rule does not appear to work beyond 1,100 years of history.

For old hedges, other features are important to dating, such as the presence of large 'stools' – the evidence of coppicing over many centuries – as well as ancient banks or walls. Maple and dogwood, which are rarely planted now, are typical of Tudor hedges while dog's mercury

Mixed hedge

is a plant known to have spread into hedges from old woodlands. The great burnet saxifrage, in southern England and the Midlands, is another reliable 'marker' of ancient hedges.

Hedge life

A hedge provides food and sanctuary for all manner of creatures. Hawthorn leaves, for instance, are the favoured food of several moth caterpillars, including the winter moth, the vapourer and the green-brindled crescent moth, while brimstone butterflies lay their eggs on the leaves of buckthorn. In the lower part of the hedge, nettles attract small tortoisehell and peacock butterflies whose larvae feed voraciously on the leaves. Where garlic mustard grows, female orange-tip butterflies will be attracted to lay.

Small rodents use the hedge for shelter and for nesting. The bank vole, ever vulnerable to the attentions of owls and other birds of prey, burrows into the soil at the base of a hedge, but may also climb it to find and open hazelnuts. Shrews also favour hedges, finding there the beetles, slugs, snails and other creatures they need to eat almost constantly to sustain their minute bodies above air temperature. Larger inhabitants of the banks at the bases of old hedges are foxes and badgers.

Hedgerow birds include the chaffinch, wren, sparrow and the hedge sparrow also known as the hedge warbler or dunnock, a bird with a most complex 'family' life that can involve partner swapping, polyandry (one female with several males), polygony (one male with two females) and even polygynandry (two males sharing two, three or four females). There is also a pecking order among the birds, with alpha males dominating and beta males attempting to destroy the eggs of a female he fancies!

The wren, one of England's smallest birds, is easy to spot from its jerky flight as it makes for cover and its long tail, held upright, as it 'freezes' to avoid detection. It is also one of the few birds that sings all year. The wren's nest is an architectural masterpiece, with grass and moss on the outside and a lining of feathers and wool within. In winter, wrens will use hedges as communal roosts where warmth can be ensured.

THE QUICKSET HEDGE

Planting live hazel or hawthorn cuttings, which quickly take root, is the way of making a quickset hedge, a term first recorded in 1484. The word 'quick' refers to the fact that the cuttings are living (as in 'the quick and the dead') not to growing speed, although it will establish quite rapidly. To demarcate parish boundaries, double hedges were commonly planted.

Tracks and Traces
How plants mark out roadside verges

Before the arrival of the motor car, the verges of England's roadsides were a kind of grassland grazed by passing beasts and constantly fertilized as rain washed their dung into the ground. A rich flora is a sure sign of an ancient verge, and there are plants found almost exclusively in such locations, including oat-grass, cow parsley, hedge garlic, wild parsnip, hedge horehound and, in spring, violets

and primroses. Most ancient of all are the plantains which, because they can withstand being trodden on, will grow through a loose road surface as well as on its verges. Analysis of pollen from old verges has singled out plantains as markers of civilization, dating back to England's earliest Neolithic settlements.

Along old cart tracks it is possible to find some rare and threatened plants including, in Cornwall, a minute rush, *Juncus mutabilis*, whose seeds will germinate only if buried then watered by moisture seeping into ruts made in the path. Similarly threatened is the mousetail, which flourishes in cattle-trodden gateways in the Fens. However new verge species are also appearing. The increasing use of salt to treat roads in winter has led to coastal plants like sea spurry and saltmarsh grass flourishing miles inland.

Marking the Miles
Guides for the traveller

To help move soldiers and supplies quickly and efficiently across England the Romans placed a cylindrical stone on their roadways after every thousandth double step, a distance of 1,618yds (1.47km). More than 50 of these still survive, many bearing nothing more than the name of the ruler of the time, but others inscribed with the distance from a town such as Eboracum – today's city of York. Although many are now in museums they can still be seen in their original locations at places such as Chesterholm in Northumberland.

Following the Norman conquest, the French mile, equivalent to 1.25 times its Roman counterpart, and throughout the Middle Ages local mile measures, were also used. The Yorkshire mile, for instance, was 2,428yds (2.2km).

Boundary and mile markers continued to be used but they

Mile marker

became much more common after 1555 when local parishes became responsible for road upkeep and again after 1593 when the mile was standardized at 1,760 yards.

From 1706 up to the 1840s tolls were charged for using turnpikes, named from the spiked barriers or toll gates through which users had to pass. From 1767 mile posts were compulsory on all turnpikes. Varying from triangular stone slabs to iron posts they were used not only to mark directions but to help calculate charges when horses were changed at coaching stations. The only items not charged for were farmers' carts and wagons and funeral traffic. Otherwise it cost sixpence for each horse and another sixpence for its carriage. To drive lambs or pigs along the road would cost a farthing per animal.

Where to Make a Wish
Passing over a stile

The stile, named from the Old English *stigel*, meaning to climb, is something to be surmounted. In past times country couples would meet at stiles to court and even take their vows. At turnstiles, wishes would be made but it was believed to be necessary, to ensure good fortune, to stick a pin into any stile over which a dead body had been lifted. It was also unlucky to put a stile on any path leading to the sea – this was sure to mean disaster to sailors.

Step stile

In most parts of England stiles are made of wood, but in Devon and Cornwall, stiles are made of stone, and may even have signs of the cross marked on them to designate them as sacred. Although no two Cornish stiles are exactly alike they come in three 'basic' designs. The high cattle stile consists of three or five treads; animals are deterred by its height and because daylight shows through the treads. The coffen stile is essentially a pit across which stone slabs are laid. The sheep stile consists of steps set into the stone face of the hedge and works as a barrier because sheep are unable to balance on the small treads.

Underground Mysteries
The secrets of limestone caves

They have been 'carved' by the forces of nature, but England's caves – virtually all of those that are inland formed in limestone – were first used for shelter by our human ancestors more than 130,000 years ago. This fact is confirmed by the dating of flints and other implements, and the discovery of fossilized remains of extinct animals such as the sabretooth tiger, which have been found at Kent's Hole near Torquay in Devon and King Arthur's cave in Whitchurch, Herefordshire, named from the belief that the monarch's bones were buried there.

Through the Iron Age and up to Roman times caves continued to be occupied, despite the fact that many were believed to be inhabited by giant demons or thyrsts, the 'baddies' of Anglo-Saxon mythology. The Romans certainly worked lead in and around the of Wookey Hole in Somerset, where the Witch of Wookey Hole 'dwells'. This crone is no more than a stalagmite, but a witch dwelling in the caves is said to have put a curse on the romance between a Wookey woman and a Glastonbury man. The man became a monk but sought his revenge, stalking the witch into the cave. As the witch hid in a dark corner, the monk splashed her with holy water, which immediately petrified her.

GRISLY REMAINS
At Gough's Cave in Cheddar Gorge remains have been discovered suggesting that its early inhabitants practised cannibalism. Marks on the skeletons appeared to have been made by flint knives wielded in systematic strokes. Alternatively this may have been some kind of pre-burial ritual.

Up and downs
Limestone caves form from the combined action of earth movements and the eroding effect of lime, grit and debris-ladened water, which also contains a weak solution of carbonic acid. Where this water drips from the roofs of caves it deposits its load of limestone, forming stalactites. Where the water drips land, stalagmites grow upwards, and the two may eventually link into a pillar. If a solution of lime trickles from a crack in a cave roof

Stalagmites and stalactites

a whole curtain can form. Colours in such structures are created by minerals like iron which makes them rusty red, copper which gives a green colour and manganese which turns them black.

Mysterious Waters
The truth about dewponds

It was once believed that England's ancient ponds were topped up overnight by dew – hence their name. It seemed almost magical that dewponds could refill themselves. In fact these artificial clay-lined ponds are replenished by rainwater and runoff from the surrounding land. Ponds were made in natural shallow basins in the porous chalk landscape hollowed, lined with clay and topped with a protective layer of flint or other stones to prevent damage from animal hooves. The linings, which set as hard as cement, have remained watertight for centuries.

Dewponds were made to provide fresh water for grazing cattle and other animals on hilltops far from rivers and streams and are commonest in the Midlands and in the downlands of the south. The pond at Chanctonbury Hill in Sussex may even have been made in Neolithic times, since flint tools of the period have been excavated nearby. Other ancient dewponds may date to the Saxon period when Oxonmere dewpond was featured in a Wiltshire land deed of AD 825, but most are 19th century constructions.

Hidden Treasure
The countryside's buried riches

Run a metal detector over an English field and something truly extraordinary may come to light! That is what happened on 5 July 2009 when Terry Herbert was metal detecting in a field in southern Staffordshire. What he found was the first of a collection consisting of more than 1,500 complete items and fragments. Immediately dubbed the Staffordshire Hoard the find includes magnificent sword fittings, part of a helmet and other military items. Most of the complete objects are made of gold, some decorated with garnet, others with fine filigree work or patterns of animals with interlaced bodies. The latest theory is that the hoard is war booty taken from fallen warriors and that it dates the Anglo-Saxon period, probably the late 600s or early 700s AD.

Also found in the hoard were three golden Christian crosses, the largest of them probably an altar or processional cross, but folded up. Whether this was to make it fit into a small space or a sign that the burial was made by pagans remains a mystery, although it is known that Christians of this period would desecrate each others' shrines. A clue may exist in another item – a small strip of gold inscribed on both sides in Latin with the quotation '*Surge Domine et dissipentur inimici tui et fugiant qui oderunt te a facie tua*', meaning 'Rise up, Lord; may Your enemies be scattered and those who hate You be driven from Your face'.

Next best

Before the unearthing of the Staffordshire Hoard, England's greatest find of buried treasure was at Sutton Hoo in Suffolk. In the early 1930s, and at various times before this, there had been talk in the area

The Sutton Hoo helmet

of 'untold gold' which aroused the interest of Edith May Pretty, owner of the estate and her nephew, a dowser, who had detected signs of the presence of this precious metal. Various small finds were made but it was only in 1939 that two Anglo-Saxon cemeteries were excavated, one of them an extraordinary ship burial – complete with a metalwork dress fittings studded with gold and gems, a ceremonial helmet, a shield, a sword, a lyre and many pieces of silver plate originating from the eastern Roman Empire. This was the burial place of a king, almost certainly Raedwald, the ruler of East Anglia.

TREASURE TROVE

Every year some 1,000 treasure hordes are unearthed in England, mostly by amateurs using metal detectors. Only five per cent were unearthed on archaeological digs. Norfolk, Suffolk, Wiltshire, Staffordshire and North Yorkshire have so far yielded the most treasure. Any finds of gold and silver more than 300 years old are Treasure Trove and must be declared and valued by the government. All such finds belong to the Crown, but finders who report and hand them over promptly are paid a percentage of their worth.

Other finds

Small finds of coins, rings and other jewellery are made regularly all over the country, dating from pre-Roman to relatively modern times. But there can be surprises. In January 2007 father and son, David and Andrew Whelan used a metal detector in a field near Harrogate in Yorkshire and discovered 617 Saxon coins and 65 other objects including a gold arm ring, silver bars that would

have been used as currency and a silver vessel probably looted from a French monastery. The entire hoard, containing items from Ireland and even Afghanistan, which had been buried in AD 927, reflects the scope of Viking travel. In 2023 a new king was added to British history following the discovery in Hampshire by dectectorist Lewis Fudge of a gold coin stamped with Esunertos, a previously unrecorded Iron age ruler. It sold for £20,400.

Living Pavements
Taking root in holes and crevices

O ver thousands of years, limestone rocks cracked and fractured during the Ice Age, have been worn down by the weather to create pavements consisting of blocks of stone known as clints separated by deep clefts or grykes. Within these grykes, and in holes in the stone, plants have managed to take root and to thrive. Even trees like ash and rowan manage to grow to sapling size in these habitats, which can be found at places such as Malham and Ingleborough in

Limestone pavement

Yorkshire and in headlands near Torquay in Devon.

As the pavements formed, grazing animals hastened the loss of soil from the rocks, which explains why it is possible to find in limestone pavements typical woodland species such as honeysuckle, dogs mercury, herb Paris and Solomon's seal in upland areas surrounded by grassland and moorland.

Limestone pavements are also prime territory for rare plants, including the dark red helleborine, a species of orchid bearing two-lipped blooms as well as the hoary rock-rose and bird's eye primrose with clusters of yellow-eyed pale purple flowers. Wild thyme, which flourishes in dry conditions, thrives here, while in places where water accumulates, ferns and mosses grow well.

Thanks to the abundance of calcium, snails thrive on limestone pavements – the only moorland habitat in which this is true. Where grass overgrowing the pavement is lightly grazed by sheep, pollen of bird's foot trefoil is collected by the wall mason bee. House martins nest on the overhanging cliffs while butterflies attracted to the flowers include bordered fritillaries, meadow browns and small heaths.

Here be Spirits?
The truth behind fairy rings

Dark green circles of lush grass in a pasture, once said to have been made by stallions, tethered goats or even the effects of lightning – if not by fairies – are in fact the work of fungi. The biggest, as can be seen on the South Downs, are hundreds of years old, several metres in diameter, and in autumn sport a 'flush' of toadstools. Sometimes other patterns form, including double and sickle-shaped arcs, but all are basically produced by the additional nitrogen which the fungal underground mycelium (a network of fine threads) releases. The fertilizer added by rabbit droppings, as on Shillingstone Hill in

Fairy ring

Dorset, is also thought to assist fairy ring production. Because rabbits crop the grass but do not eat the fungi a secondary ring may start to grow inside the original one.

According to country lore it is taboo to interfere with a fairy ring in any way, for fear of being struck blind or lame, or even being struck dead. Any boys wishing to avoid being enticed into the ring to dance with the fairies would traditionally wear their hats the wrong way round.

Puzzles in the Grass
How turf mazes are created – and why

Since long before Shakespeare wrote in *A Midsummer Night's Dream* 'The quaint mazes in the wanton green for lack of tread are undistinguishable' people in England have been creating turf mazes by cutting away the greensward to create a labyrinthine pattern. Few of these mazes still exist in England, but their remnants can be found in some parts of the countryside. That turf mazes are ancient is borne out by the similarity of their patterns to those

Turf maze

of Bronze Age labyrinths carved into rocks in Tintagel in Cornwall and to Medieval carvings like those found in churches around the country, as at St Mary Redcliffe in Bristol.

The typical turf maze is a form of labyrinth with one single path, which although it twists and turns always leads to the centre, without dead ends. Since many have the same pattern as pavement mazes in cathedrals such as Chartres it has been suggested that they had a religious purpose. Possibly penitants walked their paths whilst atoning for their sins or maybe they were used as an aid to meditation. In some places, as at Alkborough in Lincolnshire, mazes were put on village greens and used during May Day and other celebrations. At Boughton Green in Kent 'treading the maze' was part of the ritual of the summer fair, held in June each year.

Troy Town – still the name of a village in Dorset and the site of a former maze – is a name commonly associated with mazes and is also the name of one of the oldest turf mazes still in existence at St Agnes in the Scilly Isles. City of Troy, as at Dalby, near York, is also a popular name. Both are said to derive directly from the ancient fortified metropolis whose walls were built in such a complex way that any enemies who penetrated them would be unable to find a way out.

MODERN MAZES

The passion for mazes continues with modern complex 'maize mazes' created annually on farms for summer entertainment and redesigned each year, often with a theme. Seen from the air they are revealed to depict everything from a pig with piglets to a triceratops or a steam engine. At Saltash, Devon, the Duchy of Cornwall hosts an annual Halloween event in its 'Maze of Horrors'.

Sacred Waters
The story of springs and wells

Springs are the countryside's natural water supply, the source of its streams, rivers and fertility – and the reason behind the positioning of many settlements. Spring water results from a variety of geological conditions. Often, as in an Artesian well, water emerges alongside a fault in impervious rocks, allowing it to escape. Alternatively, layers of clay may trap underground water so that sheer pressure triggers spring formation. In low-lying areas, and often in valleys, the water table (the level at which the ground is saturated with water) may rise, creating a spring. In clear chalk streams it is often possible to see water bubbling up from underground.

Naturally occurring springs in England's ancient countryside, not

Village well

least because the water was pure enough to be drunk safely by both humans and farmed animals, led to the foundation of villages, towns and even cities. Exeter's original water supply came from underground springs that were utilized by the Romans in building their garrison and later by the Saxons whose minster, on the site of the present cathedral, was sited over a natural spring. Equally, spa towns such as Malvern and Bath (where the water is hot) owe their foundation to springs.

Well and good

Where water sprang from the ground, or could be reached by sinking a shaft to reach it, wells were created. But when it rose naturally to the surface it was often regarded as miraculous and as a source of health and healing. Thus springs became associated with deities (by whose divine intervention the water stayed pure) who were worshipped and presented with offerings. These, thrown into the well, ranged from coins to bronze safety pins and even shoes. The custom of throwing money into a well for luck and to make a wish come true goes back to such practices.

A DRAW FOR PILGRIMS

At the Anglican shrine at Walsingham in Norfolk, still a pilgrim destination, well water is sprinkled onto the skin of worshippers, although in former times it would be sipped – and only after a coin had been thrown into the well. A wish would then be made and a small rag or 'clootie' tied to the branch of an overhanging tree. The rags would be left to flutter, then rot over the winter, since removing them would bring about a reversal of fortune.

With the arrival of Christianity pagan well worship was discouraged and wells became saintly places of pilgrimage and healing. However the link with ancient deities persists in the custom of well dressing which still takes place, notably in Tissington and other villages in Derbyshire,

and in Upwey in Dorset. The weeks after Easter, including Ascension Day and Whitsun – the biblical feast of Pentecost – is the traditional time for the ceremony in which wells are adorned with images made from flowers, moss, ferns, coloured stones and rocks and other natural materials. Hymns are sung and prayers offered up as wells are blessed.

Bronze Age Neighbours
How the English village was founded

The English village is almost as ancient as its earliest inhabitants. Archaeological studies suggest that small communities were founded at least 4,000 years ago, this being the best way for people to cooperate and survive. Over the centuries changes in the climate, combined with the effects of waves of invasions by Anglo-Saxons, Norsemen and the Normans led to the extinction of some early villages and the re-establishment of new ones. Before land was enclosed the dwellings in a typical English village would have been surrounded by open fields cultivated in strips, arable pasture and, common land for grazing and woodland.

With the coming of Christianity, the church became the centre of the village, both materially and socially. In it, records would be kept of all village activities as well as births, marriages and deaths, plus memorial plaques and written accounts. In the Middle Ages, landowners and monasteries regularly created clearings in forests in which they established villages as a means of raising revenues from rents. For any village, however, a spring, river or some other natural source of water would have been essential.

Building to a pattern

To the discerning eye, many English villages can be seen to conform to a well-defined pattern. The 'green village' is centered around an open space, possibly with a pond or some other feature. Street villages, by contrast, tend to be much newer, often dating to the Industrial Revolution when rows of houses were built for workers, for example near streams used for the manufacture of textiles. The oldest of these villages lie along the sides of old roads used since Roman times, and possibly earlier, for transporting goods.

The village pond

For travellers, villages were places to stop for rest and refreshment, which explains why the tavern or inn remains a feature of the typical village. Many of England's oldest existing hostelries date to the end of the Middle Ages and in 1393 Richard II passed a law making it compulsory for every inn to have a sign in order to identify them to the country's official ale taster. Many early signs reflected ownership, being the heraldic badges and crests of the families on whose estates they were built and including such symbols as dragons, lions, eagles, unicorns, harts (deer), swans and boars' heads. In time, the names of monarchs were added as well as those of national heroes such as Lord Nelson.

Tyneham

Ghostly Remains
England's lost villages

They can be seen as lumps or bumps on the ground, odd lines and curves, and sometimes as pieces of stonework protruding from fields. These are the remnants of England's lost villages, ghosts of once flourishing communities, reckoned to number well over 3,000, and found in particular abundance in the North, East Anglia and the Midlands. Aerial photography continues to reveal such villages, as at Lower Ditchford in Gloucestershire.

Some deserted villages date back to the Stone Age, but many in the north were 'lost' after the Norman invasion when the armies of William the Conqueror laid waste to houses and crops and slayed people by the hundred. As a result, the Domesday

Book of 1086 recorded that more than a third of the feudal townships of Yorkshire were already 'waste' to some degree. In the 12th century the arrival of Cistercian monks, intent on establishing sheep walks and 'solitudes' around their abbeys, led to villagers being moved and their habitations demolished.

NATURAL CAUSES

Nature and the weather have been responsible for villages becoming deserted. Flooding, and coastal erosion have both played their part. Villages would also have been abandoned if springs dried up or when rivers changed their course or silted up, leaving people without access to fresh water.

The next significant change came with the great plague of 1348–9 when the population plummeted and villages that could no longer be self sufficient were abandoned, but the greatest alteration of all came in the following century when the landscape was transformed by the wool trade. Pastures once subdivided among villagers were converted into huge open areas for sheep grazing. At Glendon in Northamptonshire, for instance, the landowner evicted the 62 occupants of the village in 1514 for this reason – and in order to build a new hall for himself.

Control of the land

The rich and powerful continued to determine the fate of villages. In many places, as at Castle Howard in Yorkshire, whole villages were destroyed in the 18th century (although some were moved) in order to allow the lords of the manor to create the landscapes they desired. More recently, villages have been abandoned for practical reasons. During World War II, the inhabitants of Tyneham in Dorset moved out to make way for the armed forces, being promised by Winston Churchill that they could return once the conflict was over. They have never done so, and the village remains abandoned.

In 1935, near Sheffield, the construction of the Ladybower Dam involved the flooding of two villages, Ashopton and Derwent. Normally, the only visible reminder of these habitations is the old packhorse bridge from Derwent village, which was dismantled and re-erected at Slippery Stones. However in very dry summers, as in 1959, 1976 and 1995, the remnants of the villages become visible once again.

What's in a Name?
Tracing the roots of England's places

All over England, the names of its hamlets, villages and towns, although they have changed much over the centuries (largely in tune with the evolution of language) reflect both the landscape and the country's history, including its various conquests. The oldest of all names of which there are written records come from the pre-Roman era and derive from a Celtic language dubbed 'Old European'. Many of these relate directly to the names of rivers, such as Alcester in Warwickshire, which is on the river Alne and Porthallow in Cornwall on the river Allow.

The Roman and Anglo-Saxon legacy
When the Romans conquered England they gave Latin names to the towns most important to them. Few of these still survive in any form close to the original, but exceptions are Speen

Rivers appear as 'urn' and 'bourne' in place names

in Berkshire, whose name comes from 'spinis' meaning 'in the thorn bushes' and Catterick in Yorkshire which was originally Cataractonium meaning 'waterfall' and Manchester deriving from Mamucium, a 'breast-like hill' – probably once a significant fort. Dorchester in Dorset was, to the Romans, Durnovaria meaning 'stone the size of fist' most probably reflecting a feature of the landscape.

With the arrival of the Anglo-Saxons Roman names became altered with the language. Thus Roman Eburacum became Evorog which is much closer to York, the name of the city today. With the Anglo-Saxons came new names which still resonate today. Those containing the elements 'bottom', 'coombe' or 'dean' are named from the Anglo-Saxon word for valley, while those with 'cliff', 'tor', 'ridge, 'hough' or 'hurst' reflect the words used at the period for 'hill'. Where there were woods, names such as 'bere', 'berrow' and 'grove' were given while the presence of water led names containing 'well', 'mere' and 'pole', the last of these coming from 'pyll', a place where two streams meet.

It is no accident that so many English place names end with 'ton' since 'tun' was originally the Anglo-Saxon for an enclosed piece of land, although in time it was also used for a farm, an estate or even an entire village. In some places '-ton' transmuted into '-don', but this can also come from 'dun', the word for 'hill'. To the Anglo-Saxons a Romano-British settlement was a 'wic' – hence the plethora of names that now end in '-wick' or '-wich'.

Norman adjustments

By the time the Normans arrived in England the system of naming places was well established. Certainly names changed with the new influence of French, and some were added, most obviously in those such as Beaufront Castle in Northumberland an Belchamp in Essex, using the French words *beau* and *belle* for beautiful. Similarly Richmond and Grosmont in Yorkshire are direct translations from the French of 'strong hill' and 'big hill'.

With the feudal system came names incorporating the names of overlords, as in Caundle Marsh in Dorset and Milton Ernest in Bedfordshire. Religion is reflected in names such as Bishop's Stortford in Hertfordshire, Stoke Canon in Devon, Fryer Mayne in Dorset, Monk's Eleigh in Suffolk and Sacriston Heugh in County Durham. The immense influence of the Knight's Templar, owners of much land in England, is left in the legacy of such places as Templeton in Devon, Templecombe in Somerset and in Temple Normanton in Derbyshire.

SAME BEGINNING, MANY MEANINGS

Place names may sound similar but originate in a variety of ways. So while Minstead in Hampshire is named from the fact that mint grew there, Minton in Shropshire is from the Welsh **mynydd** *meaning mountain. Minskip in Yorkshire gets is name from the Old English* **gemaenscipe**, *a piece of land owned by the community, but Minsmere in Suffolk comes from* **mynni**, *Scandinavian for the mouth of a river. Minting in Lincolnshire, however, is named not from a feature of the landscape but from a family.*

The Perfect Roof
How thatch is cut and used

Even in the Bronze Age, which began around 3500 BC, people in England were thatching their houses. But they were not just using the straw from cereals such as wheat. Before the burgeoning of arable farming reeds, flax, sedge, broom, bracken and heather were

Thatcher

all common thatching materials, being both available and, usually, free. One of the oldest surviving thatched roofs, made of such mixed materials, still exists at Wicken Fen in Cambridgeshire and has been dated to 370 BC.

When thatch was first used farm buildings, including stables and barns such as the 11th century tithe barn at Abbotsbury in Dorset were all thatched as were churches, manor houses and other grand dwellings, including the Norman Castle at Pevensey in Sussex. In around 100 existing medieval buildings in Britain the thatch underlayer – the layer nearest the rafters – still exists in its original form.

COTTAGE STYLE

In Medieval times, the thatching of a cottage extended much farther than is usual today. This was to provide protection for the walls of the house which, being made of clay, straw and animal dung, were easily damaged by rain and snow. The outdoor privy would also have nestled under the thatch.

For many centuries a clear distinction was made between the reed thatcher or arundinator, who used the water reed *Phragmites* cut from the fens, and the straw thatcher or coopertor who employed cereal stems. In time, straw thatching was further divided into the use of 'combed wheat reed' or Devon reed, that is wheat treated to remove unwanted debris and used to give a cropped, tight reed-like finish, and 'wheat long straw' which is used untreated and produces a more flowing style of thatch.

Essential moisture

The water content of all thatch is critical. Dampness – either imparted naturally or added before roofing begins – makes the straw pliable and relaxed and, as the thatch dries, helps to ferment the sugars the stems contain. This not only deters the growth of damaging fungi, which feed on sugar, but in time also makes the straw acid, so helping to prevent attack by insects. Properly made with the best materials the thatch will become ropey and tough as it ages.

Before There Were Banks

The many uses of the barn

The original barns were, literally, barley houses, built to store the crops of Anglo-Saxon farmers. The traditional design, which can still be seen in old barns today, featured double doors opposite each other on each side leading to a threshing floor, made of oak or elm planks. Aside from convenience this placement created a draught, so reducing the amount of dust and chaff lingering in the air as the grain was threshed with flails.

The barn had other uses. Cattle could be sheltered in end bays or aisles of single-storey barns, or on the ground floor of split-level, dual-purpose buildings known in Cornwall as chall barns. These include the bank barns found in England mainly in the Lake District and parts of Cornwall, Devon and Somerset, which are built into a slope so that both floors can be entered at ground level. The

Tithe barn

lower floor provided a byre, perhaps combined with stable and cart shed.

The tithe barn dates from the 9th century, when a tax or tithe was levied on all produce from English land. The tithe's initial purpose, originally income from church property, was to hold goods in store for the poor. The tithe was paid to the rector of the parish, or to a monastery, at least until the Dissolution of the Monasteries between 1536 and 1541, after which many were passed into lay hands. Only in 1836, with the abolition of the tithe, did the need for such barns disappear, although by this time cash substitutes for actual produce and livestock had become commonplace.

BARN RESIDENTS

The barn or house swallow is aptly named from its penchant for choosing to nest where nest-building sites are perfect and insect prey ample. The mud and saliva nests are re-occupied year after year. One, with annual repairs, is known to have lasted nearly half a century.

Creatures of War
How horses came to work the land

Long before they were ridden and used for everything from personal transport to farming, England's horses – animals native to Britain – were hunted for their meat and kept for their milk. But by the first millennium BC, horses were being tethered to wheeled carts and fitted with the bronze harnesses whose remains have been found at sites such as Flag Fen near Peterborough.

Farm horses are typified by the Shire and are considerably heavier than the native breeds whose dainty direct ancestors are the ponies that can still be seen on Exmoor,

Shire horse

Dartmoor and in the New Forest. But in Medieval times, when knights started wearing heavy armour it became necessary to introduce weightier creatures from Holland, Germany and Flanders. So the Great Horse evolved and, not least because of its placid nature, also became ideal for ploughing and pulling heavy loads. Since the advent of motorised transport, numbers of working farm horses in England – not just Shires, but also Clydesdales, Percherons and Suffolk Punches – have fallen from well over a million to just a few thousand.

Revered creatures

Whatever their uses, horses were revered and the bones of dead animals were built into houses to ward off evil spirits. The brasses worn by horses, often made to represent the sun, moon and stars, were designed for the same purpose but, more importantly, to ensure the fertility of both humans and crops. In Hertfordshire, the spirit of the corn, whose presence was celebrated with the cutting of the last sheaf of the harvest, was known as 'the Mare'.

Colour was also important, it being unlucky to meet a white horse (although protection could be afforded by spitting on the ground) and extremely fortunate to encounter a piebald creature. Different parts of the horse have been traditionally used as cures. A plaited braid of hair from a horse's tail was believed to cure a goitre if worn around the neck, while one from the forelock, eaten on bread and butter, would banish worm infestations. A horse's tooth carried in the pocket would prevent and dissipate chilblains. Even foam from the mouth had a use – mixed with the juice of live crabs it was drunk to alleviate sore throats.

MEASURING THE WORK

A working horse, but specifically a Suffolk Punch, could plough an acre in a day – hence the original definition of the word. The furlong was the length of a furrow in one acre of a ploughed open field; the acre was one chain (22 yards) long, which is still the measure of a cricket pitch.

Traditional haystack

While the Sun Shines
The traditions of haymaking

It is a country truth that it is best to make hay while the sun shines. For hay that is cut when wet or green (unripe) can produce so much heat when stacked that it will spontaneously combust. Avoiding this problem means hoping for a spell of five days of fine weather in June or July and turning the hay regularly once it has been cut, a job now done by machine but once carried out laboriously by hand. The growth that follows the first cutting of hay is the aftermath, which is vital grazing for cattle.

In 'natural' hay meadows, grass grows alongside a variety of wild flowers in an environment conducive to birds, bees, butterflies and other insects. And compared with deliberately planted grass-only silage, meadows actually produce up to 40 per cent more nutrients. From the earliest days of English agriculture hay was cut with short-bladed sickles, but from Roman times these were replaced by the long-handled scythe, a tool used up to the start of the 20th century.

Dried hay was traditionally heaped into the ricks or stacks in which it was proverbially impossible to find a needle. Newly weds would sleep on new hayricks in order to ensure that they would have children, but to bring good luck it was thought necessary spit at any load of hay encountered along the road. Haymaking was once a time of feasting, when fields were divided into portions for mowing, sometimes been drawn for by lots. The whole operation was supervised by the hayward who would bring ale and food to the field for the workers. Festivities culminated with the final stacking, which in places such as Grasmere in Cumbria was attended by the village queen who rode in procession with pages and maids of honour.

Corn dolly

MANY USES

As well as fodder, hay was once strewn on the floors of homes to keep them warm and clean. Occasionally it was even used for the same purpose in churches.

With Grateful Thanks
Bringing in the harvest

On August 1st, Lammas Day, it is the custom to offer in church the first loaf of bread made from the new harvest. Originally a pagan festival its name comes from Hlaf (loaf) Mass. Even after land had become enclosed, Lammas was also the time when fences were removed so that, after the harvest, livestock could graze at large.

Before mechanical harvesting, grain was cut with sickles. This was done high up on the stem which made it easier to dry and helped to avoid cutting weeds. Once the ears had been safely stored the straw or stubble could be cut at leisure. Cutting the last blades of corn was a moment for celebration. In Hertfordshire and Shropshire, for instance, this involved 'crying the mare', the 'mare' being the tops of the last two sheaves of corn that were tied together. The reapers would throw their sickles at these, and anyone who managed to cut the knot was awarded a prize.

'Harvest home' was celebrated with processions, feasting and bonfires. At a Maiden Feast the last handful of corn was given to the prettiest girl, her dress decorated with ribbons; she was then carried home to a musical accompaniment. The last ears of corn were also made into corn dollies or 'kern babies' which were hung in the farm kitchen until the first cut of the following year, when they were ceremonially put on the fire.

Nest in the Straw
The home of the harvest mouse

There is no mistaking the spherical, grassy nest of the harvest mouse, Europe's smallest rodent, weighing no more than 6 grams (about the same as a two pence piece) and a rare sight in 21st century England due to both the growing of shorter-stemmed crops and mechanical harvesting. This home, used for breeding, is woven between the stems of wheat and other cereals and also in reed beds and similar habitats where the vegetation is dense. In winter, the creatures move underground or shelter in a different type of nest made near the ground or even inside farm buildings.

Uniquely, harvest mice are the only Old World mammals to have truly

Harvest mouse

prehensile tails, which they use to manoeuvre themselves around the cornfield. Most active at dusk they feed on seeds, fruits and bulbs, with a few insects added. At harvest time kestrels are their chief daytime predators. Year round they are preyed upon at night by owls, foxes, stoats and weasels.

The Devil's Circles
Unravelling the mystery of crop circles

Crop circles are nothing new, but have long been regarded with suspicion. The earliest known one recorded in England, dubbed the 'Mowing Devil' is depicted on a woodcut from Hertfordshire in 1678 and bears the inscription: 'Being a True Relation of a Farmer, who Bargaining with a Poor Mower, about the Cutting down Three Half Acres of Oats: upon the Mower's asking too much, the Farmer swore That the Devil should Mow it rather than He. And so it fell out, that very Night, the Crop of Oat shew'd as if it had been all of a flame: but next Morning appear'd so neatly mow'd by the Devil or some Infernal Spirit, that no Mortal Man was able to do the like. Also, How the said Oats ly now in the Field, and the Owner has not Power to fetch them away.'

More than two centuries later, an investigation by the amateur scientist John Rand Capron attributed the phenomenon to the combined effects of wind and rain, possibly a miniature tornado. Ever since then, crop circles have appeared regularly, but the phenomenon burst to media attention in 1978 when a huge number of circles, many with elaborate patterns, began decorating the English countryside. Their possible origin aroused much speculation, with theories ranging from alien invasion and UFO landings to the effects of military or intelligence institutions. Crop circles in Wiltshire, where 380 have been seen since 2005, including near Stonehenge, are thought by some to relate to the energy of ancient sites or be messages from deities such as the earth goddess Gaia.

As it turned out, the great majority of these crop circles – and those seen subsequently – were created by pranksters. In 1991 Doug Bower and Dave Chorley of Southampton admitted to making them with planks, ropes and wire. However there remain circles not made by human hand and which, if they were not formed by the effects of the weather, continue to defy explanation.

A Plague on You!
Scaring away the crows – and other birds

England's first scarecrows were not inanimate dummies but live bird scarers – boys aged nine or above who patrolled wheat fields carrying bags of stones. Whenever voracious crows or starlings landed in the fields they would chase them off by waving their arms and throwing the stones. Whether or not it was a consequence of the Great Plague of 1348, which wiped out around half of the British population, from the 14th century onwards landowners and farmers began making scarecrows, using their own cast off clothes to dress straw-stuffed sacks. A baker's peel, the pole used for moving loaves in and out of the oven, made the ideal 'backbone'. However boys – and girls – continued to patrol the fields using wooden clappers to deter whole flocks and patrolled England's fields until the early 1800s when new factories offered children better paid jobs.

Scarecrow competitions and festivals have become an English tradition with figures displayed around villages and prizes awarded. Themes include cartoon, television, historical and political characters. A leader in the movement was Urchfont in Wiltshire.

Scarecrow

At Home with the Beetles
Insect banks and farmers' friends

Running across large arable fields it is possible to find strips of tussocky, dense-looking grass and other vegetation, including flowers such as birdsfoot trefoil and white clover, organized in a series of ridges about 40cm (16in) high and some 2m (6ft) wide. These are beetle banks, deliberately created by farmers to shelter a whole range of insects, including ladybirds, wasps and harvestmen, as well as harvest mice and other small mammals. Ideally beetle banks comprise a number of different hardy grasses – typically meadow, creeping red and tall fescues, cocksfoot and timothy.

Beetle banks also encourage wildlife in general by increasing biodiversity. Skylarks can be heard singing above them, grey partridge and other ground nesting birds use them for breeding while butterflies like the small blue visit the flowering plants. Most of all, beetle banks are a boon to farmers. Violet

Fields of Blue
An ancient crop – right for today

Birdsfoot trefoil

Shimmering blue, almost like lakes, are fields of flax or linseed, England's new-but-old crop, grown today more for the health-giving oil and natural laxative contained in its seeds than for the fibres in its stems. One of the oldest cultivated plants in the world, and probably domesticated in the Fertile Crescent from at least 30,000 BC, it was grown in England for its fibres – used in everything from clothes to ropes and nets – from Neolithic times. Flax flowers, which droop and close as daylight fades, were believed in the Middle Ages to be a protection against sorcery.

ground beetles – aptly named from their iridescent bodies – prey on the adults and larvae of insects that attack grain (they will also eject a noxious fluid if handled), as do other ground beetles.

The devil's coach horse, a kind of rove beetle, consumes both caterpillars and earwigs, but also earthworms. Looking rather like a scorpion, this beetle will raise its tail when threatened and, according to country lore, in the direction of someone on whom it wished to place a curse. Killing one, except by picking it up on a shovel and throwing it into the fire, was also sure to bring about a misfortune of some kind.

Flax flower

In some parts of England, but notably Norfolk, fields of blue are likely to be lavender. Originally from the Mediterranean, lavender has flourished in England for centuries, possibly since being introduced by the Romans who used it as a relaxing addition to their baths. Lavender is renowned for its use in perfumes but also, now, for everything from the antiseptic properties of its oil to the use of its flowers as an ingredient in ice creams and other desserts.

GROWING WILD

*A wild relative of flax, the fairy flax (**Linum catharticum***) can be found in grasslands. The seeds of this small annual with white flowers, were once used as a purgative, but with notably milder effects than that of ancient alternatives such as the purging buckthorn.*

On Fire!
Why heathland is put to the flames

Whether by accident or design, fires have been breaking out on heathlands for centuries. When deliberate, their original purpose was to create extra grassland for grazing (today burning is also an important means of conservation), but by 1692 they had become such a problem that a law was passed stating that anyone found burning heath between Candlemas (February 2nd) and Midsummer would be whipped and sent to a house of correction.

Common heather

AFTER THE HARVEST

Until 1993, when the practice became illegal, stubble burning was commonplace following the harvest of wheat and barley. The aim was to kill off the seeds of weeds as well as plant pathogens and pests such as slugs, and to produce ash to enrich the soil. However the pollution created, plus the threat to mammals such as the harvest mouse, produced sufficient public pressure for the law to be changed.

On dry heath one of the advantages of fire, if it is hot enough for a deep burn, is that it destroys the humus layer that builds up under heather. As a result it exposes the mineral-rich soil essential to many heathland invertebrates such as ground beetles, burrowing bees and solitary wasps. And on dry sandy heathland with some bare and some lichen covered areas, the endangered ladybird spider is able to burrow, breed and thrive. Fire is also useful to help prevent seedlings of trees such as birch and pine establishing themselves. Left unchecked,

heathland could be transformed back into dense woodland in as little as 40 years.

Versatile Fuel
The many uses of bracken

The bracken that can so quickly grow and cover a patch of land was, from the earliest times, dried and used as a fuel, employed for thatching and, in Roman times, used as litter for both pigs and humans. It was cut for compost and, after burning, its ashes were used for making soap and even glass. So prized was it that in the 18th century, in places like Berkhamsted Common in Hertfordshire, anyone cutting bracken between June 1st and September 1st was subject to

Bracken

a substantial fine. Here, local lore recounts that bracken cutters would mass, waiting for midnight on the latter date, so as to obtain maximum gain from the harvest.

Bracken emerges in spring as aptly named fiddle heads which gradually unfurl. When other food is short it is widely eaten by grazing animals despite its unpleasant taste and ill effects, having been proved to cause vitamin B deficiency and to be carcinogenic.

Wealth on Four Legs
The history of England's sheep

The first sheep to arrive in England – probably from Europe in the early Bronze Age, around 3000 BC – were very unlike the 10 million or so that graze its grasslands today. Not only were they smaller and more like goats but they shed their fleeces naturally each summer. To make sure no wool was lost they were often penned in small paddocks so that farmers could 'roo' or pluck the wool, as well as collecting it from bushes, hurdles and fences. In these early days of domestication, sheep were valued as much for their milk – and the cheese and yoghurt that could be made from it – as for their wool and meat. A mark of this value is that sheep stealing remained a capital offence right up to the 19th century.

By the Middle Ages, when wool began to be widely exported to Europe, sheep had become vital to the English economy and in Tudor times, many merchants bought sheep farms with the express purpose of augmenting their incomes. And since a single shepherd could tend an entire flock, sheep farming was less labour intensive than arable or dairy. This led not only to rural unemployment but to wide complaints that sheep ate everything – not just the grass but whole lives too.

Modern sheep
Today's sheep, following centuries of breeding, are valued for a variety of attributes. Among the oldest hill breeds is the hardy Herdwick, named from the Old Norse for 'sheep pasture' and probably brought to northwest England by the Vikings

Black faced sheep

in the 11th century. Folklore of the Lake District once suggested that it came from a ship wrecked during the Spanish Armada. Like hill breeds, such as Cheviots, Welsh Mountains and Blackfaces, fleeces are used for everything from carpets to tweeds and knitwear. These animals are much smaller and more wiry than breeds such as Shropshires, Southdowns and Dorset Horns favoured in the lowlands, which have bigger bodies and heavier coats.

As today, when many sheep are sheared by groups of men and women who arrive each year from Australia and New Zealand, sheep were sheared in past times by travelling bands of labourers. The earliest tools were clippers that looked rather like primitive scissors. An expert shearer can take the fleeces from 200 sheep in a single day.

SHEEP LORE

The occasional appearance of a black lamb in a white flock has led to the labelling of a wayward family member as a black sheep. If, when out walking, you encounter a flock of sheep it is believed to be lucky to part them. The same action will also, it is said, cure such respiratory diseases as whooping cough and consumption (tuberculosis).

The Closest Partnership
Shepherds, their sheep and dogs

Sheepdog

Even today some shepherds still use a vocabulary that is a mixture of Old English and Latin, counting from one to ten in this way: 'Yan, tan, tethera, pethera, pimp, sethera, lethera, hovera, covera, dik'. The crooks they use – wooden shafts with a hook of iron on the end for putting around an animal's leg – have a similarly ancient past.

As well as moving sheep from place to place, the shepherd is particularly occupied with the health of the flock at lambing time. Sheep generally lamb freely without intervention, but a ewe will need assistance if the lamb is breached (turned) in the womb. At birth lambs are often born with mucus membranes covering their faces, which the ewe will instinctively clear by licking. The shepherd will assist her by removing the membranes and placing the lamb so that suckling can begin as quickly as possible.

In partnership

Shepherd and sheepdog have been a close partnership since Roman times. The border collie, the most popular sheepdog, is descended from drover dogs bred near the Scottish borders and many of today's dogs can be traced to Old Hemp, a tricolour dog born in 1893 and noted for his ability to make sheep respond to his actions. Nearly a century later another dog, Wiston Cap, born in 1963 was also widely used for breeding and can be found in the bloodlines of most of today's collies.

England's first sheepdog trials took place in 1876, not in the countryside but at a dog show at Alexandra Park in London. The result was mayhem as the dogs barked, yelped and lost control of many sheep. The winner was a common red coated working collie named Maddie, owned by John Thomas, a Welsh shepherd. Today, trials are popular events in which dogs are required to fetch, control and drive sheep, and move them into a pen or some other confined space.

Beyond the flock

Until the 17th century shepherds would officiate at weddings. They would also knit and were renowned as musicians, playing pipes made of sheep's horns or of reeds known as green corn. To pass the time, and to earn extra money, some snared wild birds while others produced elaborate woodcarvings. Shepherdesses would knit stockings. It was customary for shepherds to be buried with a tuft of wool in their hands, so that at the Day of Judgement they could be excused for failing to attend church on most Sundays.

Ancient Ancestry
The cattle of England's pastures

All England's cattle are descended in some way from aurochs, the wild oxen that once roamed its woodlands but which had already died out by the time the Romans arrived with their own dairy strains specifically bred for their milk production. These ancestral beasts were originally hunted for their meat but some 9,000 years ago were domesticated and kept not only for their meat, milk and hides but also for pulling carts and ploughs and as general beasts of burden – even on the battlefield.

The Chillingham cattle are said to be the only survivors of the herds of 'wild white cattle' that once roamed the forests of Great Britain, although genetic studies have proved that they are not related to the aurochs but descended from another ancient breed. Today these long-horned creatures can be found in a herd of around 90 individuals in enclosed parkland at Chillingham Park near Alnwick in Northumberland where they have lived uninterruptedly since the 13th century.

With the arrival of the Anglo-Saxons, new strains of cattle appeared, large in stature, red in colour and stronger for ploughing and other tasks. By the time the Domesday Book recorded the state of the country in 1086 England had 648,000 oxen which, it has been calculated, implied a total population of oxen, cows and calves of around a million. However it was only at the end of the 18th century, thanks to the pioneering work of Leicestershire farmer Robert Bakewell, that scientific crossing began, leading to the variety of breeds existing today from the Red Devon, which can weigh up to a tonne, to the tiny Dexter whose cows reach only about 295kg (650lb).

Other arrivals

As well as creatures bred locally, many other types of cattle graze the English countryside. Renowned for its prolific milk production is the Friesian, bred in Europe since the 13th century and which was brought across the Channel in 1909. More recent introductions are the Simmental, renowned for its docile nature, which was introduced from Europe for both milk and meat in 1970, and the French Charolais, which arrived in 1961 and is prized for its beef. A decade later the Limousin arrived from France. It is nicknamed the 'Carcase Breed' from its high proportion of muscle and lower quantities of bone and fat.

FOR THEIR PROTECTION

In order to protect livestock, especially in times of many deaths, it was customary to hang a dead calf in the farmhouse chimney to safeguard the rest of the herd. A live beast could even be killed as a kind of sacrifice for the same purpose, and might even be burned alive. To neutralize the power of a witch, the entrails of a bull would be charred over a fire, often in the open air.

Teeming Dung
The ecology of the cowpat

The cowpat is an extraordinary mini ecosystem on which many other creatures depend, from minute flies to birds and even bats. Within minutes of its being dropped the still warm cowpat is a target for flies which lay their eggs in the dung, using it as an incubator for their larvae which feed on dung bacteria and the nutrients that they produce. Among the first to 'strike' is the horn fly, a small insect about half the size of a housefly, which not only stays with the same herd of cows for life but has been seen to lay its eggs even before the dung has reached the ground.

Dung flies also home in on fresh cowpats, and are particularly active in spring. As they alight these small orange flies will jostle for position, then mate, following which the female quickly lays her eggs. While the larvae feed on the maggots the waiting adults settle on surrounding vegetation where they attack other insects, sucking their body fluids for food. Also attracted to soft dung are flesh flies with distinctive red eyes, striped bodies and large feet. Unusually the females do not lay eggs but deposit live maggots into the dung, which then feed on the larvae of other flies.

Within hours of being deposited, the cowpat begins to form a crust through which dor and dung beetles will burrow to lay their eggs. Working in pairs, and at night, the beetles seek out a suitable cowpat into which the female digs a deep hole from which several side chambers radiate, the male assisting her by helping to remove the excess soil and dung. As they work the beetles keep themselves fastidiously clean by grooming themselves, constantly brushing pieces of dirt from the bristles on their legs and heads. Dung beetles work similarly, the female covering each egg she lays with a protective covering of dung.

The hours of darkness are also feeding time for bats which swoop on the dung and dor beetles, and for hedgehogs which search for the beetles, slugs, woodlice and earthworms that use the cowpat for shelter. By day, jackdaws, starlings and rooks will all peck in and around cowpats for insects and their larvae. Starlings and yellow wagtails will even

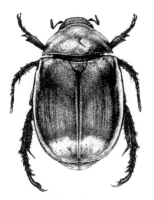

Dung beetle

perch on the backs of cattle using their position as a lookout for the arrival of flies gathering on the dung.

NUTRIENT PACKED

Cow dung is a strong fertilizer and encourages rich grass growth but can be a problem when it leaches into rivers, speeding the growth and algae and producing a thick green slime. This then inhibits animal life by reducing the amount of light that is able to penetrate.

To Eat and to Roll
Cheese – an ancient country food

Cheese making came to England with immigrants. The Beaker people, who arrived from Europe in around 2500 BC were farmers, potters and metalsmiths. The perforated clay bowls they made were used to drain the whey from sheep's milk curdled with rennet from the stomachs of suckling calves or lambs to make a hard cheese to last through the winter. This could also be salted, smoked, flavoured with herbs or honey, and might have nuts added.

Through the millennia that followed the art of English cheese making was somehow preserved and other types also made. Among the earliest soft cheeses was spermyse, a cream cheese flavoured with herbs. With the expansion of cattle herds came different varieties of cheese, each with a flavour relating to the milk from which it was made as well as the techniques used in the dairy.

'Green' cheese was not blue cheese as we understand it today but a name for very young, soft cheese like a cottage cheese, containing considerable amounts of whey. It seems that England was several centuries behind France and Italy when Stilton, its most famous blue cheese was first made, probably in the 17th century, although blue cheese was doubtless made in other places. In Dorset, the mould in Blue Vinny cheese was originally created by dipping horse harnesses into the vats in which the cheese was maturing. According to local myth, the rind of the cheese was so hard that it was once used for making cartwheels.

Beyond the table

In a tradition dating back at least 200 years, cheese rolling is a sport carried out on Cooper's Hill in Gloucestershire on the late May Bank Holiday – formerly Whitsun. A Double Gloucester weighing about 3.5kg (7lb) is rolled down the hill and competitors then chase after it. The cheese, however, has about a second's head start and can reach speeds of up to 112km/h (70mph).

Of Meat and Magic
Pigs in fact, farming and legend

Pigs have been a feature of the English countryside since at least 5000 BC when they were first hunted for their meat and for centuries wild boar roamed in England. In the

Tamworth pig

11th century, during the reign of William the Conqueror, the pig was considered so valuable that to kill one illegally was a crime. The punishment: to have one's eyes put out.

In the early days of domestication, semi-wild pigs were kept enclosed in parks – unlike deer they could not escape by jumping over fences. In both town and country they were also used for cleaning up streets and yards by eating refuse but by the 13th century they had become so numerous that in 1292 'killers of swine' were appointed to put down any stray animals.

Long before pig farming and breeding was organized, every country family would keep a pig or two. Although not exactly a pet, the pig was highly regarded, its condition carefully monitored and its health reported on in diaries and letters. Rowan garlands might even be hung around its neck to ensure that it fattened up quickly. As recorded in the Domesday Book, animals would graze in woodland, in which small areas of pasture were provided for them in clearings. Here they would feed on acorns and beech nuts (collectively known as mast), other nuts and fruits, plus bulbs and rhizomes which they would unearth with their snouts. In the New Forest people are still entitled to pannage – the right to allow their pigs to feed in woodland, heath and bog.

MARKS OF FATE
On the inner side of each pig's forelegs are five dark marks. These are said to be the marks of the Devil's claws when he entered the swine, and the reason why it is unlucky to meet a pig on the road – unless it is a sow with her litter, which foretells a successful journey. A pig's bite was once believed to result in cancer, while eating pigs' brains was thought to make people unable to tell lies – as if they had swallowed a truth drug.

Pigs of today
It was not until the 19th century that semi-wild pigs were crossed with more docile creatures from southeast Asia to create the breeds we know today, some of which are now rare. Pedigree pigs include the Gloucester Old Spot descended from hardy pigs that once foraged in the lower Severn Valley. As their name denotes they have large black spots towards their rear ends. Now rare is the small all-black Berkshire, a breed dating to the 19th century. By contrast the Large Black is much more common. Originating from both Devon and Cornwall and from Suffolk and Essex it has been used as the breeding stock for other pigs, particularly by crossing with the Large White.

The Tamworth, the ginger haired, long legged 'talkative' pig is another old breed, which originated on Sir Robert Peel's Drayton Manor Estate at Tamworth, Staffordshire as a result of crosses made in 1812 with pigs from Ireland known as Irish Grazers. It is thought to be the closest surviving ancestor of the original European forest swine. In January 1998 two Tamworths, nicknamed 'Butch Cassidy' and 'The Sundance Pig' hit the headlines when they escaped from a Wiltshire slaughterhouse, even swimming an icy river in their bid for freedom. After their eventual capture, following a week on the loose, they were re-homed in an animal sanctuary.

Piggy tales

In Dorset, the woolly pig is revered as a kind of magical animal – a ferocious wild boar with a long coat able to wreak havoc on the countryside and destroy the livelihoods of the unwary. In reality, curly-coated pigs were a Lincolnshire breed that died out in the mid 20th century. Similar Mangalitza pigs from Austria and Hungary are now being imported to the UK to prevent extinction.

Pigs might also have other powers. At Winwick in Lancashire local people believed that a pig had carried stones for the building of the church in its mouth. That pigs were so revered may date back to Celtic worship of the animals. To these ancients pork was not merely delicious meat but a gift from the gods. On a more everyday level, pigs are believed to be able to forecast rain by rushing around with straw or sticks in their mouths. Wind will certainly disconcert them – country people say that they can actually 'see' it – and they will roll in mud to keep themselves cool in hot weather.

The Fatal Triangle
A place for punishment

It is no accident that village greens are often triangular in shape, simply because they were very often created at the meeting point of three roads. In Norman times, when many such greens were created, surrounded by clusters of farms and other dwellings, they were also fairly easy to defend from undesirable incomers.

To dissipate the evil of witches and other malign influences, wych elms were commonly planted on village greens. People would take sticks from the trees and carry them for good luck while dairymaids would use them to stir their butter in their churns for fear of witches interfering with its proper 'turning' or solidifying.

The oak tree had similarly potent powers, particularly when planted at crossroads, and was also a protection against lightning. In Medieval times it would not have been uncommon to see a condemned witch or criminal hanged from a tree or a specifically erected gallows on the village green, the body being left suspended there for several days as a warning to all.

PART 2: THE LIVING COUNTRYSIDE

Things that Make Humps in the Night
How molehills are created

Afield covered in small humps – and with healthy grass – is not the work of human hand but a sure sign that, having removed most of the earthworms, moles have abandoned the site and moved on. The more scarce earthworms, and other food such as slugs, beetles and insect larvae become the more moles dig and tunnel – and the more molehills they create, but eventually they will give up, and because they rarely move far – fresh molehills will pop up not far beyond the old ones.

Molehills known as 'tumps' or even 'oonty tumps' come up overnight – even in an hour a single mole can shift 13.5kg (30lb) of soil – and will appear even when the ground is frozen as hard as concrete, simply because the animals are working below the surface on looser soil and getting rid of it through previously dug shafts. In newly cultivated fields, where the soil is soft and loose, they will make runs that look like raised ridges just below the surface. If poorly constructed these may collapse into open trenches and although they are known as '*traces d'amour*' they have nothing to do with the animals' sex lives.

In wet or waterlogged ground, but sometimes in ordinary grassland, 'mega' molehills or fortresses are constructed – large hills covered with a protective layer of soil up to 1m (39in) in height to protect against flooding. Within the fortress there is often a food cache of dead earthworms

Mole

and a nest in which young are born and weaned. Contrary to popular belief moles are not totally blind, although they are probably only able to distinguish between light and dark which is enough to prevent them from risking surfacing during the daytime.

The mole (*Talpa europaea*) gets is name from the old English 'mouldwarp', meaning 'earth thrower'. Molehills have been a nuisance to farmers and gardeners ever since land has been cultivated and to have a ring of molehills around your house is considered a sign of imminent death. However a purse made of moleskin will never, it is said, be empty of money and a mole's foot, carried in the pocket is an old cure for rheumatism.

HAPPY SQUATTERS

Abandoned molehills, in which the soil is still loose, are often taken over by mound-building ants which not only breed here but use it to store and 'farm' aphid eggs. In spring the ants release the newly hatched aphids and feed voraciously on the sweet, nutritious honeydew they produce.

Which Way is West?
How ants make and orientate their nests

So accurate is their positioning that shepherds of old would use the anthills of the industrious yellow meadow ant as compasses. The ants orientate their building to create maximum warmth, siting anthills east to west so as to catch the maximum possible sunshine. On Parsonage Down in Wiltshire, there are estimated to be more than three million such anthills, in an area of 275 hectares (680 acres), made by some 35 billion insects, with the biggest being over a century old.

In woodland, red ants build tall, dome-shaped hills, often around the bases of trees whose roots provide

Red ants

a ready-made inner scaffolding for passages and tunnels. Here, there may be 100,000 insects, even in an average-sized colony, plus larvae hatched from eggs laid in the warm, humid interior. Ants are highly protective of their nests and if disturbed will squirt formic acid at intruders. A good way to test this is to place a blue flower like a bluebell at the entrance. The acid will – like its action on litmus paper – turn the bloom pink. Ants are also fussy about cleanliness and are assisted by insects such as the hover fly whose larvae, hatched from eggs laid in the anthill, feed on ant faeces.

On the move and on the wing

Out and about, ants march along in straight lines, along trails or 'streets' up to 100m (110yds) long, which they keep clear of debris. Teams work together, paralysing caterpillars and other larvae with formic acid then either using their powerful jaws to cut up their prey before transporting it back to the nest as food for developing larvae or teaming up to transport the prey whole and intact, always using the most direct route.

This 'collective intelligence' which is also used by so-called gravedigger parties to bury their dead colleagues, is believed to work by scent.

Flying ants take to the air towards the end of July, often in vast swarms. These are winged males which emerge from the nest in pursuit of the larger, fertile winged queens. But the weather has to be just right, with warm air and high humidity. After mating the males die and the virgin queen sheds her wings before laying the eggs that will establish a new colony consisting largely of sterile females – the workers.

You Eat Me – I'll Clean You
Birds and ants working in partnership

Starlings, crows and jays can sometimes be seen standing over an anthill with their wings outstretched. They are not feeding but 'anting', triggering the insects to swarm out and squirt formic acid over their wings, so helping to kill off parasites, notably feather lice. Some birds have even been seen lying down

Jay

over the anthill and allowing ants to swarm all over them.

Green woodpeckers, however, favour anthills as a ready source of food and instead of feeding in trees have taken to using their long, strong beaks to probe for nourishment. If disturbed the birds may not fly off (they take to the air in an up and down flight like ungainly roller coasters) but will freeze for minutes on end in a characteristic posture, with their beaks pointing skyward.

From Pet to Pest
The changing reputation of the rabbit

In 12th century England, when food was scarce, rabbits, known as conies or conings, were brought from the Mediterranean to eke out the country's meagre rations. Their fur was also appreciated for its softness and warmth and to ensure the ceatures' good health and breeding coning-earths – also known as pillow mounds or conygers – were made for them, with soft soil to encourage burrowing. A few ancient pillow mounds still exist, as in Steeple Langford in Wiltshire, and at Lakenheath in Suffolk, but their traces can also be seen in the landscape, especially in places such as Dawlish Warren and Upton Warren whose names also link to them directly.

Away from the mainland, other places to find coning-earths include islands such as Lundy and the Scillies where the oldest recorded warren, dating to 1176, was made. Because rabbits loathe water and are highly reluctant swimmers, such locations were good places to confine them, and also provided freedom from foxes and similar predators. As in other locations, landowners would even insert pipes and stone burrows inside their mounds to encourage breeding.

Inevitably the rabbits broke out, but were not regarded as pests until the late 18th century. Far from it. Warrens were prized, encouraged and used commercially, as in the Norfolk Brecklands. From then onwards, however, the rabbit became increasingly regarded as a menace. It was with its extermination in mind that the myxomatosis virus was introduced from Australia, via France, in 1954 and by the end of the decade some 99 per cent of England's rabbits had died. Since then, the population has recovered and become so robust that at dusk on a summer's evening it can be possible to see more than 100 individuals in a single field.

Names and more

The warren gets its name from the Old French, meaning 'somewhere guarded' but until the 18th century the word rabbit was used exclusively for young animals, possibly from 'rabbet' the affectionate Norman French for a young individual – as we would use the word bunny today. Adults were 'conies', from the Latin 'cuniculus', a word for a burrow.

In many tales and superstitions rabbits and hares are interchangeable, but both black and white rabbits are regarded with great suspicion and black ones never killed for fear that they might be witches. Meeting a rabbit is deemed to be extremely bad luck for sailors and other workers. On the isle of Portland in Dorset, once riddled with rabbit warrens, the animal is such an ill omen that even saying its name will, it is believed, bring disaster. In times past any quarryman meeting one on the way to work would immediately turn tail for home.

Rabbit

RABBIT TALES

Watership Down, *Richard Adams' 1972 novel, is set in a real location on a hill in the north of Hampshire – a setting typically favourable for rabbit warrens which Adams observed closely. Beatrix Potter, writing in the Lake District, also made meticulous studies of rabbit behaviour before creating her tales of Peter Rabbit, the Flopsy Bunnies and other characters.*

Fact or Fantasy?
In search of England's big cats

Are they real – or just an illusion? For years farmers, walkers and naturalists have been reporting sightings of big cats roaming the countryside, and some, such as the Surrey Puma and the Beast of Bodmin, have almost become legendary. Even in October 1825 the farmer William Cobbett, famous for his *Rural Rides,* reported seeing 'a big grey cat, the size of a medium-sized spaniel' at the ruins of Waverley Abbey in Surrey.

Every year between 500 and 600 sightings are reported, including in 2023 allegedly the 'clearest ever' record of the 'Beast of Smallthorne' in Staffordshire. Convincing photographs often accompany eyewitness accounts of animals dubbed by Natural England as 'exotic, non-native and unidentified' of which 38 were big cats. Many are beyond dispute, since such animals have crossed people's paths within feet. Even without actual sightings of these creatures, the circumstantial evidence is overwhelming. In 1976, it is known for certain that following the introduction of the dangerous Wild Animals Act, which put restrictions on the keeping of certain species, a considerable number of panthers, leopards and lynxes were released into the wild.

Big cat

There is also forensic evidence. In Surrey, an eviscerated roe deer carcass was discovered and on examination was found to have puncture marks similar to those that would have been made by big cat canines, while in Lincolnshire several sheep killed and eaten had only the spine and skull remaining – typical of big cat feeding behaviour. From claw marks on dead foxes to wounds on injured horses, such clues point extremely strongly to the fact that big cats are indeed roaming certain parts of the English countryside.

... and more

Beyond big cats, raccoons – both dead and alive – have been found in the Home Counties while Siberian chipmunks have been confirmed in Berkshire, Wiltshire and Cheshire. In many parts of the country terrapins and turtles, unceremoniously dumped into canals, ponds and lakes devour fish and other wildlife and, because they carry salmonella and other infective agents, may pose a serious risk to health. Other exotic creatures that have been sighted, but not proved conclusively, include a wallaroo in Cornwall and a prairie dog in Buckinghamshire.

MISIDENTIFICATION

Everything is not always as it seems. One animal seen in Norfolk and alleged to be a big cat actually turned out on closer investigation to be a large badger.

Winter's Weather Forecaster
Can the hedgehog predict the cold?

Hedgehogs have long been believed to be able to predict storms, because they will go into hiding when bad weather is on the way. Being hibernators, hedgehogs certainly know how to predict the

Hedgehog

coming of winter and will make themselves nests or hibernaculums of leaves and moss in hedges. These are constructed with entrances at either end, and hedgehogs will seal up the one from which the prevailing winter wind arrives.

Apart from forecasting the weather, the hedgehog is thought to have other odd ways of behaving. It is said to carry apples and pears on its spines, which it will eventually eat. At night, as witches in disguise, hedgehogs are thought by some farmers to steal milk from cows by sucking at their udders. This probably stems from their habit of feeding on the insects that congregate around cowpats and other animal dung.

True to its name, the hedgehog is indeed an inhabitant of hedges and at dusk can be heard making loud snorting noises ahead of emerging from its lair to feed on snails, beetles and other invertebrates. It will also catch and eat mice and is even known to kill adders. First it bites the snake (it is immune to the adder's venom) then it stands, spines erect, as the adder continues to attack until its venom is exhausted. The hedgehog then deals the death blow. Hedgehogs are, in turn, the prey of foxes and badgers and are prone to being flattened on the roads by passing traffic. This happens because, when they hear cars approaching, their instinctive defence mechanism is to roll into a stationary ball.

Swift, Silent Killers
The owls that hunt before darkness falls

An owl flying in broad daylight? Short-eared owls – birds that favour moorlands and rough grasslands of northern England, but which live farther south in the winter months – can be seen on the wing by day. They are an impressive sight, with long wingspans and graceful flights as they search silently for small birds, bats, lizards, frogs, beetles and other insects.

Small rodents and baby birds are the favourite food of the short-eared owl and the predators are noted for congregating in areas where such food is abundant. It is even thought that in the past they were seen as an important natural pest control; in

Barn owl

1590 they are said to have rid Essex of a plague of voles that had stripped the landscape of vegetation. When they move in on the nests of crows and other birds they are frequently mobbed in a raucous display of protective parenthood. Unlike other owls, which use man-made structures, the short-eared makes its own nest, usually in a shallow scrape on the ground camouflaged by dense vegetation but, like other owls, will attack intruders, including humans. In the breeding season the males perform aerial displays such as wing

clapping to alert females to their presence; they can also offer food as bribes to win over potential mates.

In winter, when food is harder to find, other owls will come out in the daytime, including the barn owl, whose white heart-shaped face and pale underparts give it a ghostly appearance as it skims silently over the fields. What is more, such a sight has long been deemed to be exceedingly ominous – and worst of all if its daylight flight is accompanied by hooting.

Terror of the Skies
The peregrine falcon on the wing

As it dives or stoops headlong onto it's prey from a crag or treetop the peregrine falcon can reach speeds calculated at as much as 386km/h (240mph), making it the fastest creature on earth. It then strikes its victim – generally a pigeon, but possibly a black backed gull or greylag goose – with such power that death is instant. In looks these birds are also stunning, with a black 'moustache' and dark eyes. Unusually, the males are much smaller than the females.

In the days when falconry was a sport beloved of the rich and powerful, peregrines were kept and nurtured and used along with their wild compatriots whose breeding grounds were assiduously guarded. Numbers fell during the Victorian era and populations were deliberately decimated during World War II when the birds were regarded as a threat to the carrier pigeons that were vital to the war effort. The postwar use of the insecticide DDT on crops, which accumulated in the birds' eggs and thinned the shells with disastrous effects, also reduced peregrine

Peregrine falcon

numbers. In recent years, populations have recovered well and these falcons can now be found all over the country, including towns and cities. They are even used at airports, under the control of falconers, to scare off birds that threaten fatal collisions with aircraft.

Witches in Disguise?
Why hares are creatures of wonder and legend

An extraordinary sight – most likely in spring – is to see two hares standing on their hind legs and 'boxing'. This 'mad March hare' behaviour was long thought to be males fighting for dominance over a female but has now been proved to be a female warding off the attentions of an unwelcome but passionate male.

It is no accident that to run at speed is to 'hare'. To see this long-eared relative of the rabbit chasing across a field or open moorland in broad daylight is to observe one of nature's supreme movers, which can even reach speeds of 72km/h (45mph). During daylight hours hares usually crouch in their resting places or forms but will emerge to feed on both grasses and arable crops until the noise of a passing human makes them dart for cover. Unlike rabbits they are natives to Britain and not colony-makers; they live solitary lives and do not dig burrows.

In country lore it was long believed that if a pregnant woman saw a hare her child would be born with a harelip. Hares, like cats, were also thought to be witches' familiars or at worst these evil women in disguise. As a result they would be called 'puss', although this is just one of dozens of country names ranging from aunt Sarah in East Anglia to Katie in Cumberland and laverock in northern England. Only a silver bullet could, it was said, kill a 'witch-hare'. On the positive side, the Easter bunny was originally a hare, since it was associated with fertility and sacred to the Anglo-Saxon goddess Eastre after whom the festival was named.

Ballet of the Dancing Birds
How starlings gather by the thousand to roost at dusk

About an hour before dusk on winter evenings from November to March, starlings take to the skies in vast numbers. More than 40,000 birds may gather in this murmuration of birds searching for roosting places safe from the predations of buzzards, falcons and other birds of prey, many of them migrants from the near continent and beyond but all of them escaping the freezing weather in Russia and Eastern Europe.

As they swoop through the sky, wheeling and diving to prevent their movements being predicted, the birds – which have no leader except for a few seconds at a time – keep as close together

'Boxing' hares

as is practically possible so that any predator will be put off from diving into the crowd for fear of injury. Studies of starlings and other flocking birds reveal that the flock has a different leader every time it changes direction. Any bird in the group can initiate a so-called 'manoeuvre wave', which can move through the group like a ripple in any direction, from side to side or front to back. And because any bird that turns away from the flock runs the risk of being separated and being picked

off by the predator, others will not follow them. Once safely roosted the flock will sing for 30 minutes and more, then suddenly fall silent as darkness descends.

Starlings are not the best loved of England's birds, being reviled for the oily appearance of their iridescent feathers, their bullying behaviour towards neighbouring species and the damage they do to fruit crops. They will also rob thatched roofs of straw in the nesting season. However they are remarkable mimics of the calls of other birds and when flocking their squeaks and whistles are thought to help co-ordinate their behaviour.

Tracking the Midnight Traveller
Where the otter leaves its mark

The otter is a night time traveller, regularly covering several miles between dusk and dawn, and often inland from the coast. Even if it is not seen the otter will leave its mark in the form of tarry black droppings, or spraints, which it smears onto grassy tussocks, rocks and even bridge supports over rivers to mark out

Starlings

its territory. To underline its claims it will even coat the spraint with a jelly-like secretion that has an unmistakable sweet, oily smell.

Otters will also play at night, creating muddy furrows along river banks down which they slide into the water. After feeding on fish they will leave deposits of fish tails or crustacean shells. Footprints known as spurs or spoors are circular, measure about 7cm (2in) across and have five clear toe markings; a perfect print will reveal traces of the webbing between the creature's toes.

Hunting otters, creatures whose numbers declined severely in the 1950s and 60s but which are now on the increase as a result of breeding and conservation programmes, was once a popular sport, reaching its peak in the 1920s. The skins have long been held to have magical and healing properties, particularly as a safeguard against drowning and for women in labour, and as a cure for smallpox and fevers.

Nature's Gravediggers
*Exploring the community
life of the badger*

It is said by English country folk that badgers will bury their dead. Reliable witnesses of animal life have seen adults dragging corpses along tracks, taking them into the sett and covering them with earth. The 'funeral party' is even recorded as making wailing noises akin to human weeping. Such a ritual is not, however, attendant on animals unfortunate enough to lumber in front of cars and end their lives as road kill. One of the reasons that they are so accident prone may be that they instinctively follow ancient tracks which have since been 'highjacked', first by horses and carts and, now, by motorists.

Otter

Without making a special effort to observe their night time activities, badgers are rarely seen alive. They emerge at night to feed and will consume almost anything from earthworms to carrion, but they have a particular penchant for the larvae inside the nests of wasps and bees, which they will dig up with their snouts and with jaws said to be so strong that their teeth will leave a mark on a steel spade.

Badger

BADGER LANGUAGE
Recording badger sounds in Lincolnshire observer Eric Simms recognized a distinct vocabulary including grunts, barks, warning calls, threats, purrs, yarls, screams, play noises, the calls of cubs and the sounds of fights between adults.

Underground quarters
The size of a badger sett builds over many years. The oldest and most extensive have been in existence for up to 200 years with as many as 100 separate entrance holes. A complex such as this will involve shifting 25 tonnes of earth – and more. Sloping sites, such as banks, the bases of hedgerows, abandoned quarries or the old moats around ancient dwellings are particularly favoured since they drain well. Sand and chalk, rather than clay, are also chosen for preference.

Besides the main sett, which is constantly being remade and extended, badgers also make annex setts less than 150m (164 yards) from the main one, and connected to it by well worn paths. These, which are used sporadically, are often taken over by rabbits and foxes; rabbits will also share living space with badgers in the main sett, which may originally have been a rabbit burrow.

In maintaining their setts badgers are scrupulously clean and the spoil heaps they eject above ground are tell-tale signs of their presence. As well as feeding under darkness badgers regularly renew and reorganise their bedding. Fresh dry vegetation such as bracken or grass is rolled into a ball and held under the chin, pressed to the chest then taken into the sett. Most such activity takes place between spring and autumn. During the winter months badgers do not hibernate but become semi-dormant, emerging sporadically to feed in fine weather.

Thief in the Night
Saving the nightjar's reputation

That the nightjar was once believed to enter goat stalls at night, suck milk from the udders of nanny goats and make them blind, is a fact reflected in its scientific name *Caprimulgus* – *capra* meaning 'goat' in Latin and *mulgeo* 'I milk'. This nocturnal bird also has the reputation of passing deadly infections to calves during the weaning period although in fact this bird's bad press may stem

Nightjar

from nothing more sinister than the fact that it feeds on the insects that are abundant where cattle and other domestic animals are kept.

Nightjars are extraordinary looking birds with huge mouths and eyes and large pointed wings which they use in eerie, silent but erratic flight when they take to the air as dusk closes. During the day they hide in the cover of heathland and scrub (they are most abundant in southern England) where their mottled colouring affords excellent camouflage.

Nightjars lay one or two patterned eggs directly onto bare ground, and do so when the moon is full. If there is a full moon in early June, then the birds will start nesting close to that date, ensuring that when the moon is next at its maximum, the conditions will be at their best for catching moths for their growing young, which hatch only 19 days later. Some observers say that if threatened they will move their eggs and chicks from the nesting site by carrying them in their mouths.

The first sign that migrant nightjars have arrived each year, usually in May, is the haunting song of males, made from perches within their territory. Each song phrase can last several minutes, with a number of short but faster trills, lasting about half a second, during the longer trilling. These short trills, probably made as the bird breathes (which is why it can sing for so long without stopping) contain some 1,900 notes a minute.

Nature's Fairy Lights
The glow-worm's cool green sex signals

On a damp summer's evening, the flashing greenish light emanating from a colony of glow-worms is a magical sight. Contrary to its common name the glow-worm, also known as the glass worm or shine worm, is not a worm but a beetle named *Lampyris noctiluca*. The brightest glow-worm light comes from the insignificant-looking pale brown females, which have such stunted wing cases that they are virtually unable to fly. The cool light comes in a steady glow from the chemical luciferin which, when combined with water and oxygen, creates a bright green light.

As well as females, glow-worm larvae are also light producers and like the adults need damp conditions to 'perform'. Most of the glow-worm's two year life cycle is spent in this larval form; snails make up the majority of the larval diet, some of which may be 200 times each creature's own weight. Rather gruesomely they paralyse their prey by injecting a poison then sucking them dry. The larva eventually turns into a pupa before finally emerging as an adult which, because it has no mouth parts, cannot eat at all and will only live for some 14 days. It spends all this time trying to find a mate.

Light from the larvae comes in flashes, which they can keep up for hours at a time and although weaker than the light from the females is still visible up to 5m (16ft) away. The reasons why the larvae are light creators are unclear, but it seems most likely to be a way of deterring potential predators, advertising the fact that they are foul tasting.

LIGHT POWER

Insects that make light at night are even said to have been used as emergency bicycle lamps. Thomas Hardy used them in **The Return of the Native** *as the lighting for the dice game between Diggory Venn and Damon Wildeve after their lantern is put out (in an ominous portent) by a giant blow from a moth's wing.*

Creatures of the Night
The ways of the fox

In the darkness of deep midwinter sharp, intense barking, followed by eerie screams can be heard from the countryside. These are the unmistakable sounds of male foxes, fighting as they seek out females, then of the vixen before and during mating. All year round, night is also the time when foxes are out hunting for rabbits, rats, mice and – notoriously – for poultry, both wild birds such as pheasants and partridges but also the chickens kept by farmers and small holders. And the marks of a fox attack are unmistakable for after its meal it will always leave behind the skin of its victim, even that of a hedgehog.

The wily ways of the fox are enshrined in English folklore. A typical story is of the fox which, wanting to rid itself of fleas, takes some sheep's wool in its mouth and walks slowly backwards towards a river or stream. As it does so the fleas are driven towards its head and onto the wool, which it promptly drops, so drowning them. The fox is also a great opportunist. In autumn these creatures have been seen in broad daylight eating ripe blackberries and will readily take over rabbit burrows and badger setts, mercilessly evicting the residents.

Sunshine Spectacular
Moths that fly by day

It is a myth that moths only come out at night. During daylight hours many spectacular moths can be spotted in the countryside. Most colourful of the day-fliers is the dark blue and red cinnabar moth, named from the likeness of its colouring to the reddish pigment. Cinnabars are especially common wherever ragwort grows – the plant is the favoured food of the black and yellow cinnabar moth caterpillar. So much so that the moth is much encouraged by farmers attempting to eradicate this plant (see p 135) which is so poisonous to horses and cattle.

Cinnabar moth

Also splashed with red, and likely to be seen by day, are the burnet moths once believed from their colouring to be blood suckers. Most common of the burnets are the six- and five-spot types, which feed on nectar from plants such as clover, bird's foot trefoil and thistles. Clover and its relatives are also the food of burnet caterpillars which convert some of this nutriment into toxic chemicals, so helping them to evade predation from birds.

Much less conspicuous are vapourer moths, rich brown in colour, which fly along walls and windows in search of females. Also well disguised are the carpet moths, named not from their liking for household furnishings but from their subtle patterning. In deciduous woodland in March and April both the orange underwing and the very similar light orange underwing take to the air by day. And the most observant moth lover will see two tiny species of fairy moths, the long-horned moth and the metallic *Adela reaumurella*, sometimes even congregating in large numbers – almost small swarms.

Extraordinary looks

Day flying moths include some of England's most unusual species, such as the chimney sweeper which is all black but for the white fringes at the very tips of its wings, and favours bright sunshine. June or July, in grassy meadows in chalk and limestone districts are the best places to look for this now scarce moth. Even more unusual is the hummingbird hawk moth, a migrant from Europe that looks and behaves as much like a bird as its name suggests. Using its extraordinarily long proboscis to take nectar from flowers the moth hovers in the air, wings vibrating to keep itself in position.

It is the males of England's only resident silk moth, the Emperor, bearing 'eyespots' like those of a peacock, and bright orange hindwings, that can bee seen flying zig-zag fashion in daylight. Favouring moorland and open country its flight pattern is designed to pick up the scent of females when they emerge at dusk. Equally conspicuous are the caterpillars which are green with black hoops containing yellow wart-like spots.

Tiny and in Peril
How winter cold threatens the minute goldcrest

England's smallest bird – indeed the smallest in the whole of the northern hemisphere – is the goldcrest. Each of these tiny birds, striped with gold on its head as its name suggests, weighs about the same as a five pence piece. Its eggs are like small, pale pink petits pois,

Goldcrest

and are laid in a nest suspended near the end of a conifer branch, which is constructed from moss, lichens and spiders' webs, then lined with feathers. Probably because of their small size and their sedentary habits, goldcrests are particularly vulnerable to cold weather and in the worst winters as many as 8 out of 10 will fail to survive.

Welcome immigrants

In winter, Britain's resident goldcrests are joined by immigrants from Scandinavia, Poland and Russia. Occasionally huge numbers arrive on the east coast, as in autumn 2005 when bushes such as gorse and buckthorn were literally 'dripping' with them. Their nickname 'woodcock pilots' stems from the fact that they arrive, in ones and twos, ahead of the larger birds. In times past they were reputed not to fly but to ride hidden within the woodcock's feathers. Being remarkably unafraid of human contact they will, as they travel, flock around fishing boats, which gives them the alternative name of 'herring spinks'.

Almost as small, but with bright stripes across its face and, in males, an orange crown to the head, is the firecrest. These rare birds, which flutter as they feed were first recorded in southern England in 1962, since when their numbers have fluctuated, especially at Wendover Woods in Buckinghamshire where the Forestry Commission has made efforts to maintain the spruce (Christmas) trees they favour for nesting.

Omens of Death?
The lore and life of bats

According to country lore, it is lucky to see a bat flying in the daytime. But, because they are thought to be witches in disguise, these winged rodents are deemed to be extremely unlucky – and even a sign of impending death – should they enter a house. If, outdoors, bats are seen flying upwards, then this is said to be a sign that witches are convening nearby. Applied to a witch's broomstick, bat's blood would prevent her from colliding with any object; the blood was also used in black masses and in the drawing of magic circles. To dissipate the powers of a bat it is traditional to throw a hat at it.

No wonder, then, that these flying rodents are still viewed with such suspicion and dread by many, yet they are creatures with extraordinary senses, being able to find their prey by echo location, sending out high pitched sounds which bounce off insects and are detected by their highly efficient ears. Their flight, enabled by membranous 'wings', is often jerky and ungainly, hence their name of flittermice. However there is one good reason to be wary of bats. In rare instances they can carry a type of rabies virus, passed on via a bite or scratch from an infected animal, or from its saliva coming into contact with the mucous membranes. For this reason it is essential to wear thick gloves if handling a grounded or injured bat.

Horseshoe bat

Protected species

By law, all British bats are protected. Among the most endangered is the horseshoe bat, equipped with a 'leaf' of skin shaped like a horseshoe around its nostrils, and the tiny whiskered and Bechstein's bats. Most common are the minute pipistrelles which unlike most others will roost in house roofs and treetops in winter, sometimes in their thousands. Aptly, their name means 'little squeaker' and to the sharp (and young) eared they can be heard on the wing in summer and on mild winter nights when they will emerge to feed.

In woodlands, as well as parks and gardens, the brown long-eared bat takes to the wing from its summer roosts in trees and buildings. Near

water, where there is an abundance of insects, the largest bat to be seen is the noctule or great bat, the noisiest of all and a creature that is regularly attacked by starlings.

NO PLACE FOR A BAT

Bats may roost in churches but, contrary to popular belief, are unlikely to select belfries, which are much too cold and draughty. They will roost in warm buildings of any kind during summer, bearing young in these maternity roosts, then hibernate underground or in caves or mines over the winter.

Dangerous Ways
The woodcock's chancy habits

At sunset in spring, male woodcocks emerge from their woodland cover and take to the sky, flying along exactly the same route every night. As they do so they make groans and distinctive clicking sounds with their long beaks. When a receptive female responds with a call from the undergrowth, they will descend to court her. She will then make her nest in the leaves which, like her plumage, is perfectly camouflaged, and in it lay four eggs. It is no myth that once her chicks have hatched she will, if threatened, carry them out of danger by holding them between her legs.

Woodcock

During daylight hours woodcocks sit stock still in the undergrowth unless inadvertently disturbed. Here they keep watch with their black eyes which can swivel so as to provide the birds with 360-degree vision. By night they feed on a diet of worms and a few other invertebrates, but because they refuse to walk across fallen branches or other obstacles they can easily be guided into traps and snares, which is why 'woodcock' is an old name for a simpleton.

Keep Off!
How butterflies deter predators

As a bird approaches, a peacock butterfly will open its wings and, as it does so, will make a hissing noise. On its wings are bright eyespots which, as they are revealed, mimic the gaze of a predatory animal such as a cat, so effectively warning off any creature that might fancy it as a meal.

Peacock butterfly

Although not as prominent, many butterflies have eyespots on the wings, often, as in meadow browns, on the underside of the forewings. These are thought to deflect the aim of a predator away from the creature's main body. The results of unsuccessful attacks by birds can often be seen as nicks and tears in butterfly wings.

Bush cricket

Choral Evensong
The calls of bush-crickets and grasshoppers

To the practised ear the sound of any bush-cricket will immediately reveal its species. So whereas the evening 'song' of the great green (also known as the leaf cricket) is a crystalline trill, that of Rousel's bush-cricket is more like the crackle of electricity in a pylon, while the long-winged conehead produces a sound more like a light purr. Most familiar of all are the chirrups of the dark bush cricket.

Despite their name, bush crickets are more akin to grasshoppers (which also chirp distinctively according to species) than to true crickets, but make their sounds or stridulations in a different way. While grasshoppers rub their legs against their stiff forewings, bush crickets 'vocalise' by rubbing one stiff wingcase against another.

Provided it is warm enough, grasshoppers will sing during daylight hours – in a warm meadow they can be almost deafening. Both grasshoppers and bush-crickets are adept jumpers. They do this by using a kind of spring mechanism. First the legs are folded under the body, from which position it presses on the ground and takes off quickly, so achieving maximum thrust.

Bird of Good and Ill
The ways of the cuckoo

April 14th is Cuckoo Day in Sussex, where at Heathfield it was customary for a fair to be held on this day. According to local legend, an old woman carrying a basket would open it and allow a cuckoo to fly out so signalling the start of spring. The arrival of the cuckoo in England from tropical Africa has long been the moment for a whole variety of actions. On hearing the first cuckoo it is customary to turn money in your pocket (to ensure plenty for the year), to count the notes (to calculate the years until you will marry) and to look for a hair beneath your shoe (which will be the same colour as that of your spouse to be). Hearing a cuckoo before seeing the first swallow of the year is deemed to be unlucky, but hearing the first cuckoo on Easter morning is, supposedly, exactly the reverse.

While the sound of cuckoos may be welcome they are birds whose habit of laying their eggs in other birds' nests is legendary and has spawned words such as 'cuckold' for a spurned husband. Literally within seconds of alighting on the nest of its host – one of 50 different small insect-eating birds but most commonly a pied wagtail, sedge warbler, meadow pipit, or reed warbler – the female cuckoo will deposit an egg that looks remarkably similar to the clutch already laid there. The exception is the dunnock, whose eggs are blue and is thought to be a much more recent host than the other birds.

Cuckoo

Even before this the female cuckoo will have carefully surveyed the nest to establish the laying habits of the female she is about to dupe and, moments before, will have used her beak to remove a newly-laid egg, thus doing all she can to allay suspicion. Once the cuckoo chick hatches it will push any of its host's eggs or young unceremoniously from the nest and the unwitting foster female will work tirelessly to feed a young bird with a huge brightly coloured and imploring gape which, in just a fortnight, will be three times her size.

A dying breed

Cuckoos in England are a dying breed. Since the 1980s they have declined by 75 percent, leaving a total of 15,000 breeding pairs in Britain. Woodland areas are the most affected. The birds may be suffering because habitat destruction and the increasing use of herbicides are reducing host populations, but more significant is the fact that, due to a warmer climate, these birds are nesting earlier, which pushes cuckoo egg laying out of synch with that of its hosts. Add to this fluctuating supplies of moth and butterfly caterpillars caused by unpredictable weather, and continuing droughts in Africa where the birds winter, and the odds against cuckoo survival continue to mount.

Before the migratory habits of the cuckoo were known and understood it was believed to turn into a sparrowhawk during the winter months, or to hide in hollow trees. This reputation was enhanced by the fact that because it feeds largely on caterpillars its innards were thought

to be so hairy and indigestible that it was never preyed on by other birds.

NOT FROM A BIRD

Cuckoo spit – the white 'froth' that appears on grass and other stems in early summer – is not produced by the bird, nor does it, as was once thought, conceal the baby animal spat from the mother's mouth. In fact it is made by the larva of the froghopper (a small insect, technically a bug) which, after it hatches, sucks the sap of the plant which is then mostly extruded from its rear end, along with air bubbles and a sticky liquid, so providing it with a protective covering while it develops.

Good Enough to Eat – and Drink
Treasures of the edible countryside

It is well known that dandelions and nettles are edible, but the English countryside has dozens more delicious greens and salads on offer. Some of these would now be classed as weeds, but in times past the concept did not really exist for tasty plants such as these. As a bonus, many also have medicinal properties.

For adding a mild garlic flavour to salad the crinkly leaves of Jack-by-the-hedge or garlic mustard (*Alliaria petiolata*) has been used since Medieval times, if not longer. In the 16th century the herbalist John Gerard, called it 'sauce-alone', saying that the leaves should be crushed and eaten as a sauce for salt fish. In country places it was often chopped and mixed with vinegar and sugar, then eaten with lamb in the same way as mint sauce.

TREAT FOR THE YOUNG

The young leaves of the hawthorn or May have the country name of 'bread and cheese', not because they taste of these ingredients, for in fact they have a nutty flavour, but because they were once the first wild vegetable eaten by children. Medicinally, hawthorn leaves have been proven to benefit the circulatory system by expanding the blood vessels and allowing more oxygen to reach the heart.

Greens for cooking

Waste ground all over England is abundant in fat hen or all-good (*Chenopodium album*), which has probably been a staple food since prehistoric times – certainly its remains have been found associated with many ancient settlements. Its old name was melde from which, it is thought, Melbourne in Cambridgeshire is named, as is Milden in Suffolk. The plant's alternative name of muckweed comes from its propensity to flourish in or around dung and compost heaps.

Fat hen is best cooked and eaten like spinach, and the same goes for

Fat hen

the foliage of its close relative, Good King Henry (*Chenopodium bonus-henricus*), whose remains have also been found in Neolithic sites. It may even have been actually grown as a crop, having been introduced to England from Europe by Bronze Age settlers. Its name denotes both its excellent qualities and its favourable comparison with 'Bad Henry' or dog's mercury, which is poisonous.

Although loathed by gardeners for its invasiveness, ground elder or goutweed (*Aegopodium podagraria*) has tasty, tangy leaves when cooked. Brought to the country by the Romans it was cultivated as a vegetable and also sold at the roadside, from inns and monasteries, as an 'instant' remedy against the agonizing pain of gout.

Pudding grass, one of the many country names for bistort (*Persicaria bistorta*) is evidence of the way in which the leaves were traditionally used – made into a pudding with oatmeal, onions, nettles and seasoning (some recipes also include blackcurrant leaves, dandelions or barley). Dock pudding is still made in the Calder Valley in Yorkshire – a region where the plant grows abundantly in upland meadows – and eaten as an accompaniment to bacon and eggs. Bistort also has the name of 'passion dock' from the fact that the pudding was made and eaten during Holy Week, its bitter taste recalling Christ's passion and death.

Mallow, whose leaves are full of mucilage, was also brought to England by the Romans, and used both as a nutty-tasting vegetable and a medicine. In the pot it makes a soup similar to maelokhia, an Egyptian dish to which meatballs may be added, creating a texture similar to that of okra. Medicinally the dried leaves are used to treat inflammation of the respiratory, gastric and urinary tracts, and of the eyes and skin, as well as coughs, asthma and bronchitis.

LEAF LIQUEUR

Young beech leaves not only have a sweet flavour and silky texture when eaten raw but in the Chilterns are traditionally made into a potent liqueur. They are first steeped in gin, then the resulting bright green liquid is strained off and sugar and brandy added.

Pretty but Deadly
*Poisonous plants and
how to spot them*

Benign though the countryside may seem, danger lurks in river bank, hedgerow and wood in the form of poisonous plants and fungi, threatening both unwary humans and grazing animals. Arguably most poisonous of all is hemlock (*Conium maculatum*) a tall umbellifer reaching 2m (6ft) in height, which favours damp ditches and riversides. It is best identified by its purple-spotted stems and, when the foliage is crushed, its rank mousy, sour smell. Causing respiratory failure and paralysis, before death finally ensues, hemlock is notorious for being the poison supposedly administered to Socrates at his execution although it loses its potency when the stems get old and dry.

Twining up the hedgerows is the poisonous deadly nightshade (*Atropa belladaonna*) which, following its purplish flowers, bears shiny black, succulent berries packed with the chemical hyoscamine. If eaten, these will inevitably result in paralysis – as few as three berries have proved fatal to children. This nightshade is often confused with the red-berried woody nightshade (*Solanum dulcamara*) whose fruits, though they taste intensely bitter, will not deal a death blow.

Hyoscamine is also the poison contained in henbane (*Hyoscymus niger*), the plant allegedly chosen by the notorious Dr Crippen to kill his wife in 1910 (thanks to DNA analysis the whole story has recently been questioned). Nonetheless henbane, a plant whose grey-green leaves are covered with sticky green hairs, needs to be treated with great caution. From the shape of its seed heads, which resemble molars, these were once chosen to treat toothache, although they are more likely to have produced hallucinations than pain relief.

Much prettier is the blue flowered monkshood (*Aconitum napellus*) whose blooms look like monks' copes, and which can occasionally be found in woodland. In Medieval times the plant moved from countryside to garden where it was cultivated for use as an arrow poison for hunting animals as well as a painkiller. But the plant is so poisonous that even touching it can be dangerous, resulting in heart failure.

DANGEROUS BERRIES

Many attractive autumn country fruits need to be treated with extreme caution. Berries of holly, spindle and yew are all poisonous. Also deadly are the bright red berries of the cuckoo pint or lords and ladies, borne in clusters after the sheath around the brown flower spike has faded. Come Christmas, mistletoe berries may bring romance but must never be eaten.

Poison in Wood and Field
Fungi to treat with extreme caution

Of the thousands of fungi that appear in England each year, probably only about 20 are actually deadly, but some are to be avoided at all costs. Most aptly named is the death cap (*Amanita phalloides*), an innocuous looking specimen which, if eaten, has a mortality rate of between 50 and 90 per cent, causing vomiting and diarrhoea followed by liver failure, intestinal bleeding, mental torment and death. Growing in beech and oak woods it has a pale olive-yellow cap with mottled markings and fibres radiating from the centre. The stem bears a large, dangling ring near the top while the base is not only swollen but sits in a kind of bag, known as a volva.

Other relatives of the death cap share its nasty qualities but are more easily recognized. Among them are the fly agaric (*A. muscaria*) the 'fairytale' toadstool with its white

Death Cap

spotted red cap, and the panther cap (*A. pantherina*) which is similarly spotted but with a chocolate brown cap. The destroying angel (*A. virosa*) is a ghostly white colour. Its tell-tale sign is that the volva covers the entire body of the fungus. Its ill effects are due to amatoxin which, if treatment is not administered, can destroy the liver and kidneys within 24 hours. Consuming as little as half a cap is all that is needed to produce fatal effects.

Less well known are two other fungi with appropriate names. The deadly fibrecap (*Inocybe erubescens*), found in pastures as well as deciduous woodlands, is a cream-coloured fungus whose distinctive radial fibres turn red with age and whose cap often splits at the edges. The great danger of this fungus, whose intrinsic chemical muscarine affects the nervous and digestive systems, is that when young it looks very similar to a button mushroom. The deadly webcap (*Cortinarius rubellus*) is more easily identified, but is a rusty reddish orange in both cap, gills and stem and bears yellowish scales. Pine and spruce woods are where it is most likely to be encountered.

To Cure the Sick
Wild flowers with healing powers

It is no accident that the wildflower *Euphrasia officinalis* has the common name of eyebright. For centuries this plant has been renowned for its ability to treat inflamed eyes – a fact now proven by the extraction from it of substances called iridoids which do indeed act as anti-inflammatories. Eyebright also contains tannins, which improve resistance to infection, and phenols that slow the growth of infective bacteria. And as well as helping the eyes, this semi-parasitic plant, which grows on chalky grasslands and meadows, will help clear catarrh when taken as an infusion.

All over the English countryside there are dozens of plants with medicinal properties, effective if used with caution. Along with eyebright other anti-inflammatories include blackberry, marsh mallow and coltsfoot. Rosebay willow-herb, renowned for its ability to colonize bare ground, and the first flower to bloom on bomb sites in World War II, has the additional benefit of being able to soothe digestive problems, a boon for which peppermint has been long renowned, and for which mallow, mugwort, meadowsweet and angelica are all effective.

A stronger heart, better sleep

It had been known by the ancient Egyptians that the foxglove, although poisonous, has the power to strengthen the heartbeat. However the plant's true potential was realized only in the 18th century by the English doctor William Withering who used the dried leaves (now known to contain the substance digitalin) to cure the symptoms of congestive heart failure. To help prevent problems of the heart and circulation, doctors today recommend antioxidants, as found in blackberries, rosehips and bilberries.

As well as being used to flavour ales and beers since the Middle Ages, dried hops have long been put in pillows to help improve sleep. The essential oils and resins they contain have a distinctive, slightly yeasty aroma. An infusion of dried hops, which has grown wild in England for millennia, can work even more effectively when taken before bedtime. Valerian is another old sleeping remedy – in this case it is the underground rhizomes that contain the essential ingredients for calming the nerves, lowering blood pressure and so helping to alleviate insomnia.

For the skin – and more

Putting a dock leaf on a nettle sting is an excellent temporary remedy for the irritation, but there are other wild flowers that can do even better things for the skin. From medieval times, poultices of burdock root were used to treat wounds, boils and other

Foxglove

skin complaints, and to ease the pain of rheumatic joints. It was also old country practice to make creams and lotions from plantain leaves to soothe chapped skin, insect bites and grazes. The flowers of red clover have a similar use, but with the additional advantage of being able to help relieve everything from gout to sore throats and ulcers.

CANCER RESEARCH

On the trail of new drugs to treat cancer, mistletoe has been singled out as a distinct candidate, since it contains substances that have been found to inhibit the growth of tumours. As yet, these are too toxic for practical use, but research continues.

Relics of the Past
Woodlands in history

Some 7,000 years ago, after the end of the last Ice Age, England was covered almost entirely by woodland and contained all the broad-leaved trees that are familiar today, including birch, beech, oak, hazel,

ash, hornbeam and sweet chestnut. As the human population expanded the woods were gradually cleared, both for agriculture and for building, but how this was done is still a mystery, since trees are in fact very hard to kill. Unless their roots are actually dug up from the soil they have a remarkable ability to regenerate – as proven by the practice of coppicing. Some trees may have been destroyed by fire, while the stumps of felled trees may have been prevented from regenerating by the browsing of goats, sheep and cattle.

In the centuries that have followed woodland has been successively cleared and replanted but England has never again been so densely forested. However it is estimated that at least a quarter of the woodlands recorded in the Domesday Book still exist today. It is possible to experience this ancient woodland at places such as Wychwood Forest in Oxfordshire, Rockingham Forest in Northants, Grovely in Wiltshire and Micheldever Wood in Hampshire.

Two of the most spectacular old woods that still thrive are at opposite ends of the country. At Wistman's

Wood on Dartmoor, named from a local word for 'wizard' or 'wise man' is a fragment of an old oak wood, a collection of gnarled, stunted old trees growing high above sea level, trailing with lichens. Although none is a specimen of the original trees that first took root between 6,000 and 7,000 years ago, after the end of the last Ice Age, all are their direct descendants. In County Durham, the trees of Castle Eden Dene ravine, known as the 'jungle of the north' directly reflect the vegetation of the same period and is a tangle of ash and wych elm, with many yew trees also prominent.

LITERARY SETTING

The wildwood was used as the setting for early literature, notably the story of King Arthur and the quest for the Holy Grail, in which it is uninhabited except for the occasional hermit in a wayside chapel who could offer shelter and advice to a weary knight. While wolves and bears would have roamed it in reality, the tales feature only beasts such as white harts, lions and the fictional unicorn.

Legends in Their Boughs
England's mighty oaks

The oaks of England are its 'signature' trees. Most are the descendants of the trees that clothed the landscape some 7,000 years ago and some are a millennium old – and more. Their wood has been used for everything from ships, beams, timbers and floors to gates and pews. Oak is so hard that it is impervious to the effects of alcohol, making it the ideal choice for beer, cider and wine barrels. Acorns, the fruits of the oak, have long been used to feed pigs and other domestic animals and, in hard times, even humans too. The bark,

Mature Oak

which is rich in natural tannin, was once harvested for tanning hides and hollowed out trunks were country people's coffins.

Not all oaks are the same, and it takes a keen eye to distinguish them. England's most dominant oak is the common or pedunculate oak (*Quercus robur*) which carries its acorns on long, slender stalks. Also widespread is the sessile oak (*Q. petrea*), more likely to be seen in the west and north of the country, away from chalk, whose acorns have very short stalks. The Turkey oak (*Q. cerris*) is easily distinguished by its bristly, shaggy acorn cups and darker, more slender leaves; it grows most abundantly in woods and parks.

Old oaks have a remarkable ability to survive despite the fact that with age fungi such as the sulphur bracket fungus colonize its wood, developing from spores that penetrate through breaks in the branches and similar wounds. In time the fungus sends its threads deep into the tree's heartwood which becomes decayed; then the weight of the upper branches, aided by the force of the wind, splits the trunk. Many of the branches

subsequently die off, giving the tree a ghostly appearance, but it can continue to live for many decades.

Teeming with life

It is estimated in that in an average life of around 250 years a single oak tree and its immediate surroundings may be 'inhabited' by more than 200 different types of organisms. Magpies and squirrels use it for nesting and decaying and softened wood is ideal for woodpeckers and owls. Even the spaces between the roots can make ideal dens for foxes. Mosses, algae and lichens, as well as ivy and mistletoe, live on its trunk and branches.

An oak tree also teems with insect life, which makes itself obvious in a variety of ways. The caterpillars of the oak leaf roller moth, which are laid in the tree's trunk in late summer and hatch just as new leaves are emerging in spring, decimate the foliage. Fortunately most trees are able to survive such attacks by growing a second flush of leaves. Golden brown discs on leaf undersides are the hallmarks of the appropriately named silk-button gall, created by the reproductive efforts of a type of cynipid wasp. The oak apple, too, is the result of insect activity. After the female gall wasp lays her eggs in a young oak shoot a spherical gall forms in which the larvae develop. Old galls bear the tell-tale holes indicating that these have matured and emerged.

The sacred tree

It was beneath the oak's spreading branches that the wizard Merlin is believed to have worked his enchantments and because of its associations with the gods is said to be the first to be struck by lightning in a thunderstorm – farmers still plant oaks near buildings to act as lightning conductors. At Yule, the ancient ritual from which many of our Christmas customs derive, an oak log was always chosen as being the most likely to draw the sun back to the earth. To the Druids, whose name means 'oak men', the tree was – and is still – revered as sacred, and thought to embody the spirit of their god Esus. The mistletoe, which occasionally grows on it as a semi-parasite, was believed to guard the tree from evil. Cutting it with a golden sickle on the sixth night of

the moon will, they believe, preserve its magic.

THE OLDEST OAK

The Marton Oak of Cheshire, reliably dated to be at least 1,200 years old, is probably the oldest uncoppiced tree in England although it is split through the middle as a result of natural decay, which probably began in the 18th century. In the past 200 years its girth has been measured several times and before the split, so records say, the trunk was a massive 17.6m (58ft) in diameter. Every autumn, the acorns are gathered and sold for 10 pence each to the benefit of the local church.

Trees in Danger
Diseases that threaten England's landscape

In the half century from 1940, more than 25 million of Britain's elm trees were killed by Dutch elm disease, caused by two related species of fungi of the genus *Ophiostoma*, carried from tree to tree by beetles. But now new diseases are threatening other trees, threatening disaster of equal proportions.

Acute oak decline, caused by a bacterial infection, can kill an oak tree in just a few years. In an affected tree, likely to be more than 50 years old, dark fluid seeps from cankers – cracked areas of dead bark – and runs down the trunk. In time, the canopy thins and the tree dies. Oaks – but more usually other trees, notably larches and beeches – are affected by sudden oak death. The culprit is the fungus *Phytophthora ramorum* which infects and is harboured by rhododendrons, plants that have escaped from gardens and rampaged across the countryside. As a result huge efforts are being made to remove rhododendrons from places where they threaten the health of woodlands.

Ash dieback, which probably originated in Asia, was first found in England in 2012. Also caused by a fungus, namely *Hymenoscyphus fraxineus*, it has already killed thousands of trees by blocking water transport within the plant, leading to dead branches, blackened stems and crown dieback. Spread by the wind, it is easiest to spot in high summer when trees begin losing leaves. Fortunately many have natural resistance.

Ancient Markers
The plants of England's oldest woods

It is possible to discern the presence of ancient woodland by the plants that grow beneath the trees. Many of these woods will also have been coppiced, so allowing enough light in beneath the leafy canopy in spring to encourage flowering plants to thrive.

Sheets of bluebells in an English woodland are a wonderful sight, and a hallmark of old, coppiced woodland.

Wild bluebell

In times past, when forests were places full of evil enchantment, it was thought that they rang out their bells to summon fairies to gather – although any human hearing them would soon be struck dead. On a more practical note, bluebell bulbs, being full of toxins, were used to make a glue for bookbinding that was immune to attack by silverfish. Medicinally, the bulbs are an ancient source of both diuretics, which act on the urinary system, and stypics, which will stem bleeding. When not growing beneath trees, as in open heathland mixed with bracken, bluebells are a sign that the land was once wooded.

For bluebells to thrive they must be protected from trampling (by farm animals and humans), and must have water without being waterlogged. Light is essential, too. Given such favourable conditions bluebells will spread quickly, both by seed and by producing offshoots from their bulbs. However the survival of the true bluebell is threatened by the more vigorous and highly fertile Spanish bluebell, a garden species with which it hybridizes freely.

Since Neolithic times, or so it is thought, wild garlic has been eaten both as a vegetable and as a flavouring for other foods. Also known as ramsons or stinking onions it has given its name to many places including Ramshorn in Staffordshire, Ramsey in Essex and Ramsbottom in Lancashire. Wild garlic woods were earmarked as boundaries in English land records going back to the 1st century AD. The plant is so vigorous that it will essentially blot out all other species in an area until the extraordinarily pungent leaves die down in June.

Woodland rarities

One of the strangest looking plants of ancient woodland is Herb Paris, also called the true love knot. Each plant has four broad leaves, held flat to the ground, topped by a flower consisting of a 'crown' of four narrow green petals and four wider green sepals. The whole is topped with eight long, golden stamens. Later in the season a single large, shining black berry appears which was once revered as a deterrent to witches, hence its alternative name of devil-in-a-bush.

The wild lily of the valley or ladder-to-heaven is becoming increasingly rare in woodlands. This British native will grow only where plenty of shade can be assured and where the soil is poor – sandy and acidic locations are ideal. Like other plants of old woodlands wild lilies of the valley were once renowned for their medicinal properties including their power to treat apoplexy. Dried flowers were also used like snuff to clear the head.

The 'Everlasting' Tree
The life of the small-leaved lime

Centuries of coppicing, in which trees are cut down to leave stumps or stools from which new, straight shoots then grow

Small-leaved lime

and are cropped, is an English country practice that can prolong the life of a tree almost indefinitely. This fact is nowhere more true than at Westonbirt Arboretum in Gloucestershire where a massive stool of a small-leaved lime (*Tilia cordata*) measuring more than 16m (52ft) across has been calculated by radiocarbon dating to be more than 6,000 years old. The tree has other natural attributes that promote its longevity, being able to survive severe cold and the crowding of its roots and branches within a hedge.

The small-leaved lime or linden was once a common tree of the woods that carpeted England and its name is reflected in many Anglo-Saxon place names such as Lyndhurst and Linwood in the New Forest (although it no longer grows there). Where it does persist – in Devon, the Mendips, the Wye Valley, Essex, Lincolnshire, the Derbyshire Dales and the Lake District, it is the practice of coppicing that has assured its survival.

As well as being used for fencing poles, coppiced lime shoots were stripped of their bark and the inner, fibrous material used as ropes. Soft and pale, lime wood has long been favoured by wood carvers, most notably Grinling Gibbons who used it for such works as the choir stalls in St Paul's Cathedral.

The Tree with Mystic Powers
The ash tree in life and legend

It is an ancient belief that the ash tree has the power to heal – and more. An ash branch, charred at the end and drawn in a circle around a sore on the skin will, it is said, effect a cure, while it is an old country practice to pass a sick child through a split made in the trunk of an ash. The tree was also observed to heal itself as recovery took place, the effect being particularly curative for ruptures and weak limbs. According to country legend the ash confers protection against snakes which, it is said, will not creep over a circle of the tree's leaves placed on the ground. Equally, if an ash twig is used to draw a circle around a snake on the ground the creature will, supposedly, die of starvation.

Ash trees, like oaks, were frequently planted near buildings in order to attract lightning and also had the ability to protect against the damage of storms and the powers of witchcraft. But to harm an ash tree can be dangerous, bringing bad luck and disasters of all kinds. These attributes of the ash may well arise from the fact that its wood is immensely strong, smooth and supple, being used for the handles of tools and weapons of every conceivable kind. Nowadays, however, the ash

Common ash

is not valued as much as in the past, particularly because its seeds – borne in 'keys' that float on the wind – germinate easily into fast growing plants that quickly take over open spaces in woodlands and grow as unwelcome weeds in gardens.

Branches of Holiness
How the yew tree became sacred

It is no accident that yew trees can be found growing in more than 500 English churchyards. Long before the arrival of Christianity this tree was specifically selected for planting in burial grounds for his ability to protect against evil, to symbolize everlasting life and to purify the departed. While many yews are contemporary with the medieval churches alongside which they grow, a significant number are much older. To cut down a churchyard yew, or even to burn or damage it in any way, is believed to presage ill fortune, because sprigs of yew were once put into a dead person's shroud and branches carried by mourners before being put into the grave with the coffin.

Yew

More practically, yews were probably planted in churchyards because they were poisonous to cattle but yet highly desirable for their wood, which was used for centuries to make longbows. Yew was also invaluable for spears. One such weapon, found at Clacton in Essex, has been dated to 250,000 years ago; it is the world's oldest known wooden artefact.

Away from human habitation, yew grows in woodlands alongside trees such as beech, maple and ash, favouring well-drained chalk and limestone soils. Trees are either male or female, the latter developing poisonous seeds each surrounded by an innocuous bright red fleshy covering, the aril. Thrushes and other birds are able to eat the whole fruit without ill effect because the seed passes through their intestines without being digested.

Living Meat?
The extraordinary beefsteak fungus

In just 14 days in late summer or early autumn a massive fungus up to 30cm (1ft) across, looking exactly like a piece of meat, can appear on the trunk of an oak or sweet chestnut tree. This is the beefsteak fungus which is reddish brown in colour with a rough hairy surface and, on its underside, small yellow pores. Even more oddly, the fungus will 'bleed' a red juice if it is cut or damaged, making it look even more like its namesake, but although it is not poisonous, the fungus tastes insipid and not at all like meat. As a result of fungus growth, the wood of its tree

Beefsteak fungus

host becomes dark brown in colour. This so-called brown oak is greatly valued by furniture makers.

The 'Magic' Carpet
Life in the leaf litter

As the leaves fall from the trees of a deciduous woodland in autumn, an amazing 2kg (4lb 6oz) of spent vegetable matter is deposited on every square metre (sq yd) of the woodland floor. Almost miraculously this does not accumulate into some vast pile, but is broken down by fungi, bacteria and myriad invertebrates, most of them hidden from view (either because they are too small or are most active at night), creating a rich layer of humus beneath the surface which, year by year, disintegrates to form a deep, loamy soil underlying the whole.

Of all the creatures that consume leaves and churn the soil, earthworms are the most adept, some of them burrowing as deep as 2.5m (8ft) below the surface. And they are present in their thousands. One estimate puts their numbers at over 135,000 per hectare (2 acres). A variety of earthworm species are hard at work in the woodland floor, including England's biggest, *Lumbricus terrestris*, which is able to fix its tail within the burrow and retreat rapidly from the hungry jaws of the badgers, foxes and birds for whom it is a prospective meal. Small red brandlings or tiger worms also abound in leaf litter.

COUNTRY NAMES
Earthworms have a variety of colourful names in different parts of the country including angle-ditches, dew-worms, lobs, night crawlers, rainworms, yeth-worrms and woggans. Because they are often seen early in the morning following rain, it was once thought that earthworms fell from the sky.

Also vital to leaf consumption are the springtails, tiny six-legged insects which can bound through the air like fleas using a special organ at the back of the abdomen. Believed to be among the first animals to conquer the land some 400 million years ago, they are able to survive extreme cold and cluster in leaf litter in huge numbers, possibly as many as over 435 million in a single hectare.

Many legs

Millipedes abound in the woodland floor. While their name means, literally, 'a thousand feet' most have fewer than 50, although the blunt-tailed snake millipede has as many as 200. Their food is

Woodlouse

decaying plant matter, ideally leaves or wood that has already been worked on by bacteria and fungi to rid it of harmful tannins and make it both safe and easy to digest. They are expert tunnellers, but if disturbed will either coil themselves up or, if they are pill millipedes, roll into a ball.

Woodlice – also known by dozens of different names including hog-lice, pill pigs, tiggy-hogs, shoemakers and lockdoors, are equally adept at curling up when discovered lurking under rotting wood and leaves. Just to stay alive these creatures, whose digestive systems contain cellulose-busting bacteria, need to eat between 5 and 10 per cent of their body weight every day and as well as munching

vegetable matter will eat their own faeces in which this first food is part digested.

Small invertebrate carnivores of the woodland floor are the centipedes, (occasionally with over 100 legs but more usually around 30) which use their poisonous claws to trap woodlice and other similar creatures. They hunt by detecting the scent of their prey and by sensing its vibrations, moving their legs in rhythmical waves to get up speed in the chase. Also on the hunt for prey are beetles and the pseudoscorpions, which use their huge claws to capture smaller invertebrates before devouring them.

Fighting for a Mate
Stag beetles in combat

With 'antlers' locked, male stag beetles use their huge mandibles to fight each other and so commandeer the most favourable mating sites. These increasingly rare and now protected insects are residents of England's woodlands and need dead wood to complete their lifecycles. After the male has mated with the female (she is distinguished by her lack of 'antlers') she lays her eggs underground in logs, or in dead tree stumps. Here the larva will spend from three to seven years, slowly maturing within a large cocoon that can be as large as an orange, before emerging as a fully fledged adult which will then mate and die shortly afterwards.

Stag beetles have mixed reputations. In the Middle Ages they were depicted as companions of the Madonna and Christ child, and thought to have the power to defeat evil and ensure salvation. In country places, however, they were frequently blamed for fires in hayricks and thatched and dubbed 'Devils' imps'.

Trials of Strength
The life of the deer

In autumn, the sight of male deer rutting is awesome indeed as stags whistle, roar and charge at each other, then lock antlers in a tussle of strength to determine which will mate with the does. And because the females are fertile for only a single day each year, the competition to mate is enormous. Genetically the winner's prize is massive, for he will mate with as many females as possible. Having large antlers is a huge advantage and in red deer the best endowed males have branches with as many as 10 points. A stag with 12 such points is dubbed 'Royal'.

Red deer, inhabitants of Exmoor and the Quantocks in England (but also widespread in Scotland) are native to Britain. Until the Middle Ages they were widespread over the country, giving their name to

Stag beetle

Red deer male

roe deer, typified by their white rumps and simple antlers. Known to have lived in England since the Mesolithic (10,000–6,000 BC) they became extinct there as a result of overhunting in 1800. During the Victorian era they were reintroduced from Scotland and Europe, since when they have thrived. They can be seen at woodland edges and in cornfields during daylight hours and anywhere at night. Being ruminants they spend much time resting and chewing the cud. The bucks (males) rut in the same way as other deer, but usually in late summer.

places such as Hartfield in Sussex and Hartanger in Kent. But as woodlands were cut down to provide timber for shipbuilding and the like, and as they were hunted for sport and for venison, numbers declined and the fallow deer, a native that died out during the last Ice Age but was reintroduced, probably by the Romans, took its place in parks, estates and the countryside.

Roaming the countryside

The deer that can be seen in the countryside, and which are becoming an increasing menace to farmers and country gardens, are

ALL IN WHITE

The original white hart, one of the emblems of Richard II was probably not a deer but an antelope of some kind. According to legend the original White Hart, after which many pubs are named, was an animal called Albert which was hunted by Henry VII in the New Forest. Rather than being killed the creature is said to have been given a gold collar – as still portrayed on the inn sign at the White Hart inn at Ringwood in Hampshire.

Feeding Frenzy
The spectacle of the mayfly

On a sunny morning in late spring or early summer, when the hawthorn or may blossom is in flower, a massive, frenzied swarm of winged flies can be seen shimmering over a river or stream. These are mayflies which, during June as well as May, emerge in vast numbers, bringing on a feeding frenzy in trout, salmon and other fish and delighting the most amateur of anglers. Indeed the mayfly season is known as 'duffer's fortnight', and when mayflies are not in season expert anglers do all they can to create flies which resemble them as closely as possible.

Aptly, the name of the mayfly, also called the dayfly, has come to be associated with the ephemeral, for the adults live only a day or two – just long enough for them to mate and for the female to lay her eggs. But the complete mayfly lifecycle is considerably longer. The resilient eggs survive over the winter, hatching in spring into nymphs which, sometimes for another whole year, feed on algae and other vegetation on the river bed and moult to replace their skins up to 20 or 30 times as they grow and develop. Finally, they emerge as brownish winged juveniles which are the food so favoured by fish. Then the mayflies develop very quickly. Within hours they change into shiny winged adults, which then mate and die.

In the story of evolution, mayflies were one of the earliest insect species and the only insects to have two different winged forms within their lifecycle. Mayfly fossils have been reliably dated to over 300 million years, long before dinosaurs appeared.

The Record Breakers
Heavyweight freshwater carp

In June 2010 anglers mourned the loss of one of England's largest known carp. Known affectionately as Heather the Leather, the fish, which weighed 23.6kg (52lb) and was

Mayfly

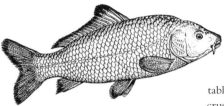

Common carp

about 50 years old, was a scaleless leather carp, a subspecies of the common carp (*Cyprinus carpio*). It had been fished for over 30 years and caught, on average, three times a year, in a lake in Yateley in Hampshire. In August of that year the mirror carp Two Tone, aged over 40 and weighing a massive 38kg (67lb 14oz), died of natural causes at Conningbrook Kent. The current official angling record is for a carp caught in 2016 at Wasing, Berkshire by Dean Fletcher. It weighed 39kg (68lb 1oz).

Carp were kept for food by the Romans in their home country (they came originally from Asia) but they probably first arrived in England in the 1300s and were kept in stew ponds before being eaten for their firm flesh. They gradually migrated into rivers from lakes and fisheries on the large estates of the wealthy

and, because they can survive from long periods out of water, became much loved by anglers wanting to fish for sport rather than for the table. The fish feed by sucking up crustaceans and other invertebrates from the mud and are reported to make loud slurping noises at night, a habit that also makes their flesh muddy tasting.

A relation of the goldfish, with which it is able to interbreed, the crucian carp is a totally different species than the common carp. Native to Britain, it is widespread in southern counties. In contrast to 'true' carp it has no barbels or feelers, has golden or red fins and grows to only 45cm (18in) in size.

They Walk on Water
Amazing adaptations of pond life

They really do walk on water! Pond skaters skid over the surface of ponds using water repellent hairs on their legs to stay 'afloat'. These hairs are also extremely sensitive and able to sense vibrations and movements on the water surface.

A small fly or any other insect falling into the water will create ripples that reveal its whereabouts, triggering the skater to dart across the water to capture and consume its prey.

A twig that walks – not a figment of the imagination but the mobile home of maturing caddisflies. The adult female lays her eggs in or near water which, when they hatch, develop into 'architectural' larvae. Using pieces of sedge, twigs or stones as building materials they bind these together with silk spun from their bodies, often chewing vegetation to make it more malleable and decorating their homes with pieces of shell.

When a larva gets too large for its case, it first moults, then builds another larger case to grow into. Only when fully grown does the larva attach its case to a reed or stone in the water. It then seals itself within until the fully developed pupa emerges as an adult.

The caddisfly is named for the caddisman, a pedlar who roamed the countryside. He was often a cloth salesman who advertised his wares by wearing strips of brightly coloured fabric or yarn. The name may also link to the caddy or box traditionally used for storing tea.

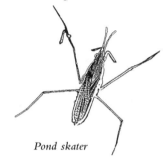

Pond skater

Swimming and diving

A snake swimming across the still water of a pond or river is an extraordinary sight. This is no water snake, but a grass or ring snake, distinguished by the yellow collar or ring around its neck and its olive green back marked with vertical black bars along its flanks. Agile swimmers and, despite their name, never found far from water, grass snakes hunt for toads, frogs, fish and newts. Unlike adders, grass snakes are not poisonous. If threatened they will feign death and, if picked up, will hiss, bite and squirt a foul fishy-smelling liquid from the opening of their intestine.

LOVE NEST

A silvery ball beneath the water – a miniature diving bell – is the shining 'love nest' of the water spider. Here it will retreat to eat its prey, and will mate and lay its eggs. Within the bell this 'scuba spider' is even able to monitor the quality of the air. When carbon dioxide levels rise too high it will replenish stocks by carrying in bubbles of air which it traps on the long hairs covering its legs.

Nests under water? Seen in the shallows these are not the work of birds but of male sticklebacks who, by secreting a glue, stick together pieces of plant leaves and stems, along with grains of sand to make nests. To lure a female the male, as well as showing off his building skills, also develops bright red throat markings and bright blue eyes. Once tempted into the nest to mate, the females lay their eggs which the male fans with his fins to supply them with the oxygen essential to their development.

Threatened by Cultivation
Rare flowers of the countryside

Around the English countryside wildflowers abound. And apart from orchids there are several rarities that any plant hunter would be thrilled to find. In meadows, one of the rarest is the snake's head fritillary or chequered lily (*Fritillaria meleagris*), also known as Lazarus bell and leper lily because its square-patterned flowers are shaped like the bells that lepers were obliged to carry in Medieval times. Where they do grow abundantly, as in North Meadow, near Cricklade in the Thames Valley, about

Fritillary

a tenth of the blooms that appear from March to May will have white heads and there will be rare double-flowered heads too.

In Oxfordshire, the only county where fritillaries are found in any numbers, they are still celebrated on a Fritillary Sunday. Today the event is centred around the plant conservation but in the past, when the flowers were more abundant, Fraucup Sunday (from a local name) was the day on which they were picked in quantity and sold, often for charity. In Staffordshire, at Wheaton Aston, the most northerly site of the wild fritillary, a similar fritillary wake is held.

The demise of the damp-demanding fritillary, which is not native to Britain and may in fact be an 'escape' from Tudor gardens, has declined through the draining and ploughing of meadows and the use of land for gravel extraction. In places where it is preserved it is protected through a return to the old practice of designating 'Lammas Land' on which haymaking is delayed until July and on 12 August (Lammas Day in the old calendar).

Herbicide victims

The widespread use of herbicides is almost certainly responsible for the demise of the pretty annual pheasant's eye (*Adonis annua*) adorned with brilliant scarlet flowers like small anemones and feathery leaves. The plant is named for the handsome Greek hero from whose blood it is said to have sprung after he had been killed by a wild boar. In days when it was much more common in the cornfields of England the flowers were gathered and sold in Covent Garden market as 'red Morocco'. Today, however it is restricted to just 18 sites in southern and south-east England, always on chalk. Kiss-me-quick or corncockle (*Agrostemma githago*) was also abundant and easily distinguished by the way in which its purple petals are folded like a flag before they open. Before the use of herbicides its abundance was due to the fact that its seeds were 'harvested' with the cereals in which it mingled and were inadvertently sown again in the next season.

The corn buttercup, also called Devil-on-all-sides, scratch bur or hellweed, on account of the vicious spines on its seeds heads, is another victim of modern agriculture, having once been common but unwelcome in cornfields where its seeds would contaminate the harvest. Much prettier but equally endangered is the wild cornflower – it has not been seen painting whole fields with its blue blooms since the 1920s. However the introduction of set aside has helped reinvigorate natural cornflower populations. And when topsoil unaffected by herbicides was used to create Pitstone Nature Reserve in Buckinghamshire, taken from an old chalk quarry, it was found to contain dormant seeds of cornflower, corncockle and pheasant's eye, which continue to bloom there.

POISON AND CURE

Although all parts of the corncockle plant are reported to be poisonous it was used in the past as a remedy for all kinds of ills, from parasitic infestations to cancer. The cornflower is traditionally used to help the eyesight – it is said to be particularly effective on blue eyes – and for treating inflammation of the kidneys, for gout and for rheumatism.

Black Gold
Precious peat and where to find it

For the past 360 million years, plants growing in wet, acidic areas of England, including Lancashire, Cheshire and East Anglia, have been dying, decaying and becoming transformed into peat. Foremost among them is the ancient sphagnum moss, the feathery moss familiar to gardeners (and used in hanging baskets) which grows in large cushions and is able to absorb several times its own weight in water. Present on earth eons before flowering plants evolved it has helped to create a unique environment described as our 'rain forest' because it stores vast

Sphagnum moss